WOMEN IN
ALCOHOLICS
ANONYMOUS

Recovery and Empowerment

Jolene M. Sanders

FIRST**FORUM**PRESS

A DIVISION OF LYNNE RIENNER PUBLISHERS, INC. • BOULDER & LONDON

Published in the United States of America in 2009 by
FirstForumPress
A division of Lynne Rienner Publishers, Inc.
1800 30th Street, Boulder, Colorado 80301
www.firstforumpress.com

and in the United Kingdom by
FirstForumPress
A division of Lynne Rienner Publishers, Inc.
3 Henrietta Street, Covent Garden, London WC2E 8LU

Library of Congress Cataloging-in-Publication Data
A Cataloging-in-Publication record for this book
is available from the Library of Congress.
ISBN: 978-1-935049-08-1

British Cataloguing in Publication Data
A Cataloguing in Publication record for this book
is available from the British Library.

This book was produced from digital files prepared by the author
using the FirstForumComposer.

Printed and bound in the United States of America

The paper used in this publication meets the requirements
of the American National Standard for Permanence of
Paper for Printed Library Materials Z39.48-1992.

5 4 3 2 1

WOMEN IN ALCOHOLICS ANONYMOUS

I would like to thank all those women who participated in the survey that made this research project possible. Their candor and honesty are reflected throughout this work, shedding light on the recovery process and spreading hope to other women who may be suffering from alcoholism.

Contents

List of Tables		*ix*
Acknowledgments		*xi*

1	Introduction: Why Alcoholism Is a Feminist Issue	1
2	Women and Alcoholism	21
3	Women in Recovery	45
4	Women's Struggle with Surrender: Steps One through Three	67
5	Women Cleaning House: Steps Four through Nine	81
6	Women Passing It On: Steps Ten through Twelve	97
7	Conclusion: Empowering Women, Collectively and Individually	115

Bibliography	*135*
Index	*141*
About the Book	*145*

Tables

2.1 Summary of demographic variables that describe women in AA, the AA Membership Survey, & the U.S. Census (percent)   25

2.2 Summary of the problems experienced by women in AA (percent)   31

3.1 Comparison of the length of time in AA between women in AA & the AA Membership Survey (percent)   47

3.2 Frequency of attendance at AA meetings by women in AA (percent)   48

3.3 Summary of reasons to attend women-only AA meetings by women in AA (percent)   50

3.4 Summary of helpful activities engaged in by women in AA (percent)   57

3.5 Seeking help outside of AA by women in AA (percent)   62

4.1 Working Steps One & Three: Level of difficulty experienced by women in AA (percent)   73

5.1 Working Step Four: Level of difficulty experienced by women in AA (percent)   83

5.2 Working Step Eight: Level of difficulty experienced by women in AA (percent)   91

6.1 Summary of Eleventh- & Twelfth-Step activities engaged in by women in AA (percent)   100

6.2 Comparison of religious affiliation between women in AA and the General Social Survey (percent)   108

6.3 Comparison of the belief in God between women in AA
    & the General Social Survey (percent)   110

6.4 Comparison of other religious indicators between women
    in AA & the General Social Survey (percent)   112

7.1 Comparison of gender roles between women in AA &
    the General Social Survey (percent)   117

7.2 Comparison of feminist indicators between women in AA
    & the General Social Survey (percent)   120

7.3 Summary of the top five feminist activities engaged in by
    women in AA (percent)   122

7.4 Summary of other good things experienced by women
    in AA (percent)   124

Acknowledgments

Although there is only one author's name on the cover, this book would not have been possible without the contributions of many people, and it is fitting to take this opportunity to express my gratitude. First of all, I would like to thank Esther Ngan-ling Chow. Her engagement and efforts as a feminist teacher, researcher, and advocate have inspired my own. In addition, her advice and direction were instrumental to the final shape of this research project. I am deeply grateful to have had her guidance and example along the way. A special expression of thanks is due to the 167 women from AA who agreed to participate in the survey. Their willingness, especially in the qualitative sections of the questionnaire, to re-examine their oftentimes painful pasts in order to share their "experience, strength and hope" constitutes the *sine qua non* of this study. Their profoundly hopeful stories of transformation from the darkness and despair of alcoholic powerlessness to the light and freedom of empowered existences provide the breadth and depth of meaningful information found in this book.

I would like to thank Thomas F. McGovern, editor of *Alcoholism Treatment Quarterly*, for his encouragement and support. Portions of this study were first published in his journal, and he strongly encouraged me to publish the whole work. His very positive, professional assessment of the value of this study affirmed my faith that this inside view of women in Alcoholics Anonymous and how they work the Twelve Steps constituted a significant contribution to the field. I would also like to thank Andrew Berzanskis for his careful editorial guidance in bringing this project to fruition in its current form. In addition to shepherding a novice author through the technical process of preparing a manuscript, he too recognized the value of this study in feminist empowerment and provided crucial support to my effort to get this unique perspective into the hands of those who share an interest and concern about women in recovery from alcoholism.

Finally, I would like to thank my family. My daughter, Brooke, and my son, Joe, have patiently endured Mom's absences, either researching the study or cloistered in my office writing it. My husband, Tom, has supported me unconditionally during this long odyssey. He encouraged my study, advised me to find a research project I was passionate about, and has been there throughout, as my first and last reader. He is my number one supporter. This project would not have been completed without their love and support.

1
Why Alcoholism Is a Feminist Issue

This book examines a group of women in recovery from alcoholism in order to further understand the nature of recovery from such a devastating disease. Initially thought to be solely a man's disease, alcoholism and problem drinking now afflict at least 4 million American women aged 18 years or older, according to recent studies (Grant et al. 1994). Although it has devastating effects on men and women, alcoholism tends to cause more harm to women because of the physiological, psychological, and sociological differences between women and men. While some progress has been made, treatment of alcoholism continues to be informed by the male perspective, which has acted as a barrier for some women who have sought treatment for alcoholism (Walitzer and Sher 1996). Even a voluntary organization like Alcoholics Anonymous (AA) that exists to help individuals recover from alcoholism continues to be perceived as a "male–only" club although one third of its membership is now made up of women. Finally, there remains a lack of research specifically about women and alcoholism by experts in the field of addiction treatment (Beckman 1994; Copeland and Hall 1992; Worth 1991). If no longer completely inaudible, the voice of the woman alcoholic remains muted. For all of these reasons and my concern about how feminism has viewed the subject, I have conducted the following research in order to highlight from a feminist perspective what is working and to encourage more women so that they too can recover from alcoholism.

It is ironic that alcoholism has been conceived of as an exclusively male problem, because the physiological effects of alcoholism are actually far more severe for women than for men. Due to physiological differences, 30 percent more women than men develop cirrhosis within two years after the onset of heavy drinking (Wilsnack, Wilsnack, and Miller-Strumhofel 1994). Moreover, because women have more body fat and less water in their bodies than men, alcohol enters a female's system in a less diluted state and causes more immediate harm. For example, women tend to get intoxicated faster than men and are quicker to develop alcohol-related diseases (McCaul and Furst 1994). The progression of alcohol dependency develops faster in women. Hence, although women begin drinking alcohol at a later age than men, they seek treatment for alcoholism at approximately the same age as men (Lex 1991). More alarming is the fact that the death rate for alcoholic women is 50 to 100 times greater than that of alcoholic men (Van Den Bergh 1991). In fact, alcoholism is now the third leading cause of death in women between the ages 35 and 55. Additionally, it is estimated that alcoholic women lose as much as 25.9 years of life and their average age at the time of death is 51 (Pape 1986). There is no doubt that the innate physiological differences between women and men and the different way that the female body metabolizes alcohol leave women with more health risks and a greater probability of death due to alcoholism than men.

Another issue of great importance is how alcoholism affects the pregnant woman. Fetal alcohol syndrome and effects (FAS/E) is a very serious consequence of alcoholism among pregnant women. Research shows that thousands of newborns continue to be at risk of incurable birth defects because of the alcohol consumption of their mothers (Jacobson and Jacobson 1999). Links to other problems, such as dyslexia, learning disabilities, and minimal brain damage, are now being made to alcohol consumption on the part of pregnant women, as well (Royce and Scratchley 1996).

In addition to more severe physiological issues, women also suffer from more severe psychological problems related to alcoholism than do male alcoholics. For example, alcoholism in women has frequently been associated with such psychological problems as depression related to life histories of victimization. Up to 25 percent of women seeking treatment for alcoholism are diagnosed as suffering primarily from depression and only secondarily with alcoholism (Beckman 1994). In such cases, women use alcohol as a response to their depression. Furthermore, depression, which has been estimated to affect one in six women, has been significantly associated with women who have histories of physical, emotional, and sexual abuse. Several clinical studies conclude that women with addictive diseases are over-represented in the population of women reporting abuse histories and that sexual abuse is more common than not among alcoholic women (Langeland and Hangers 1998; Miller and Downs 1995; Wilsnack et al. 1994). Such data link past sexual abuse to depression, alcoholism, and in some instances, to both. It is clear that women alcoholics experience multiple forms of victimization. As a result, they suffer from severe psychological problems, in addition to their alcohol addiction.

Although not all women who become alcoholics have a history of victimization, women alcoholics have more pronounced problems with self-image and self-esteem than do male alcoholics. Many women in recovery report feelings of low self-esteem and worthlessness, which contributed to their substance use. These women used alcohol to mask feelings of inferiority and continued to use alcohol in attempts to feel whole or complete. In fact, one recovering female alcoholic, Jean Kirkpatrick, believed so strongly in the underlying lack of self-esteem in female alcoholics that she initiated her own program of recovery in 1975 called Women for Sobriety.[1] Kirkpatrick attributed low self-esteem in alcoholic women to the social stigma attached to alcoholic women, to shame experienced by alcoholic women, and to the guilt alcoholic women often feel about their addiction (Kirkpatrick 1977). Studies of Women for Sobriety and AA suggest that negative feelings generated from stigma, shame, and guilt deter women from seeking treatment and make it harder for women to recover, once in treatment. Perhaps as a result of these compound factors, the recovery rate is still low relative to the number of women who are active alcoholics (Plant 1997). Hence, I believe it is necessary to understand both the properties in recovery that block and discourage women from seeking treatment, and those elements in recovery that are conducive to sobriety among women alcoholics. The following is a beginning toward this end as I look specifically at AA from a feminist perspective.

Second-Wave Feminism and Its Perspective on AA

According to second-wave liberal feminists—those who identify with the American and European feminist movement of the 1960s and 1970s—feminist empowerment is a combination of feminist consciousness and feminist activity. During the second wave, the more radical strain of feminists brought women together in small groups, so that they could educate women about the fact that they have been treated as second-class citizens who have been oppressed based solely on their gender. These groups called consciousness-raising groups were short lived but effective. The mainstream liberal feminist movement still remembers and values the role that consciousness-raising groups played in the advancement of second-wave feminism. This more radical activity helped to springboard the second-wave feminists into collective action that was and still is associated with liberal feminist thought and praxis.

The liberal feminists worked within the democratic structure to effect social change for women. Their primary goal was to create equal opportunities for women through political and economic reforms.

Activists in this tradition used the law to promote equity among men and women based on the principles of self-interest, equality, and individualism. Also, because liberal feminists viewed gender differences as socially constructed, they advocated changes in gender socialization to promote equality among men and women. In general, liberal feminists believed that changes could be made in the existing social order to facilitate feminist liberation.

Women who identify with liberal feminism and especially the more radically oriented are likely to harbor criticisms of AA. For example, liberal feminists with radical leanings do not accept the idea that an organization can be apolitical, because from their point of view, if the organization is not actively fighting for women's rights, then it is simply upholding the status quo of discriminatory practices against women. This orientation leads some feminists to view AA skeptically, because AA explicitly states that it is not aligned with any "sect or denomination, nor do we oppose anyone." (Alcoholics Anonymous 1976, xiv).

In addition to concern over the lack of active political involvement by AA as an organization, liberal feminist critics of the twelve-step movement argue that the emphasis on spiritual development as described and practiced in the twelve-step model is not compatible with feminist consciousness. As previously discussed, this feminist critique of the twelve-step movement considers women in recovery to be subjugated by patriarchal influences (Berenson 1991; Kirkpatrick 1986; Rapping 1996; Tallen 1995; and Walters 1995). These feminists view the traditional, Christian-based principles practiced in the twelve-step movement as complicit in the promotion and reinforcement of traditional gender roles for women and the general submission of women to men. Also of concern to liberal feminist critics is the twelve-step movement's practice of encouraging personal change and spiritual enlightenment through self-reflection and a belief in God or a "higher power." Feminist critics view this method of personal development as backward and harmful to women as compared to the second-wave feminist methods of self-reflection tied to political activism. Overall, this particular feminist critique believes that the recovery movement represents a backlash against their own agenda, which emphasizes that the personal is political, that women are oppressed under traditional religious practices, and that structural changes are necessary to liberate women. These feminists hold strong second-wave feminist beliefs that empowerment comes from a feminist consciousness developed through collective political action. Thus, these critics view women who participate in the twelve-step programs as stuck in a "myopia of self-absorption" (Rapping 1996, 13) and as unconsciously contributing to the backlash against the feminist movement.

The feminist critique of the twelve-step movement described above is a predictable reaction given that the feminist impulse to empower women has traditionally been associated with the political. Beginning with the first wave of the feminist movement in the United States, women fought for and gained the right to vote through collective organization. As a result of their collective action, women empowered themselves through the impact of the individual vote now enjoyed by all women. Similarly, second-wave feminists empowered themselves through political organization, winning civil rights legislation for women and other significant legislation, such as Title IX giving women equal access to education. Liberal feminists also came very close to securing ratification of the Equal Rights Amendment (ERA) to the United States Constitution. In general, the American feminist movement is most noted for its political action and unprecedented success in advancing women's social positions.

General Feminist Concerns about AA

For those second-wave feminists who still believe strongly that the feminist project should influence public policy, implications of treating alcoholism among women from a feminist perspective are numerous and significant, because a thorough feminist analysis will look at the effect alcoholism has not only on the individual woman, but also on the family and the larger social system in which the alcoholic woman lives.[2] Alcoholism in women is not an isolated problem. Women who have been raised in dysfunctional families—in this case, a family harmed emotionally, psychologically, and spiritually by addictions—often repeat patterns of dysfunctional behaviors within their own families, perpetuating the cycle of addiction, chaos, and despair. It has been well documented that women who experience abuse as children often marry abusive men (Fagan 1993; Miller and Downs 1995; Pan 1994). Furthermore, women who have been raised in alcoholic families have a greater likelihood of marrying an alcoholic or of becoming an alcoholic (Miller, Downs, and Gondoli 1989). Additionally, several studies have documented the positive correlation between parental abuse of alcohol and subsequent use by teenage and adult children (Ulman and Orenstein 1994; Weinberg et al. 1994; Windle 1994). Moreover, because there exists a social stigma regarding alcohol and drug abuse, families with addiction problems tend to deny or hide their problems. In such families the rule of thumb is to not communicate, to not share intimate emotions, and to not challenge the status quo. Often children reared in such environments, in addition to participating in recovery programs, seek psychological counseling, because they do not have the emotional or social skills with which to effectively express themselves. Family-systems therapy has recognized that one member's addiction can have a profound effect on the whole family. Enhanced understanding of women's experiences with alcoholism and recovery will further promote the movement toward framing addiction and treatment in a more holistic picture that is also consistent with a feminist perspective.

Although alcoholism and addiction can be traumatic to members of an alcoholic family and to the family unit as a whole, recovery can be equally empowering. As a result of the pivotal role that women have traditionally played in families and that they continue to perform to this day, an enhanced understanding of women alcoholics and their recovery experiences will have enormous implications and applications in areas of public policy dealing with families. In the same way that practicing alcoholics influence other family members to abuse alcohol, once one member in the family seeks recovery from an addiction, other family members become more likely to seek treatment as well (Schaef 1986; Davis 1997). Moreover, families in recovery are able to develop a language through which they can identify their dysfunctional behaviors and work toward healing. Women, in particular, are given the opportunity to restore relationships with their spouses and children. Similarly, children of families in recovery have a far better chance of not repeating the cycle of problem or alcoholic drinking that their parents experienced. Because women are so often the center of families and the ones responsible for the moral and emotional well-being of families, it is imperative that the feminist analysis of women in recovery seek to understand the family system and its contribution to the recovery process.

In addition to understanding the relationship between women, their families, and the recovery process, feminist researchers have begun and need to continue to focus on the relationship specifically between public policy, on the one hand, and the opportunity for and availability of treatment for women, on the other hand. For example, because the current federal alcohol and drug initiatives favor policies in line with the "war on drugs," a disproportionate amount of attention and funding goes toward crime and punishment rather than toward treatment and recovery. Of those few dollars from the federal alcohol and drug programs spent specifically on women and their families, much is applied to cover the costs of mandatory treatment of pregnant substance-abusing women. In this context, treatment serves as a form of social control, and the therapeutic process is compromised by the conditions set forth by the state. Furthermore, public policy initiatives need to address the obstacles women face in seeking treatment voluntarily. For example, in addition to needing help with substance abuse, women seeking treatment in federally funded treatment facilities often tend to be single parents who lack job skills and who need help with transportation, child care, and housing (Blume 1997). In such instances, case management and other social services are necessary to facilitate the therapeutic process. Given the conditions which hinder women's entry into the recovery process, it is essential that feminist researchers assist in educating policy makers about the recovery process and how it is affected by the conditions and circumstances under which women seek treatment.

AA as a Feminist Locus

One of the primary places for women to get help for their alcoholism is AA. Current estimates of AA membership put the size of the organization at "more than 105,000 groups and over 2,000,000 members in 150 countries."[3] The 2004 membership survey found that 35 percent of AA members are women (Alcoholics Anonymous 2004). That means that there are almost 700,000 women in AA around the world. By any measurement, this is a substantial and significant form of organization and action by women attempting to recover from alcoholism.

It is my contention in writing this book that feminist scholars, students, and the general public need to understand AA and the experience of women in it, precisely because of its significance for women alcoholics. Yet AA as an organization and as a culture of recovery is widely misunderstood. Alcoholics Anonymous defines itself as a voluntary organization that offers a program of recovery from alcoholism based on its Twelve Steps. According to AA, the Twelve Steps are suggested practices that enable an alcoholic to resist the compulsion to drink and to build a better way of life, based on a spiritual awakening that results from working the Twelve Steps. This spiritual awakening is little understood by outsiders and in fact AA offers only a very general description of what a spiritual awakening is.[4] Although membership figures indicate that women have carved out their own niche within AA, feminist observers of AA still have concern over the role of the Twelve Steps in women's recovery. Given that they are the central ingredient of AA's recovery philosophy, feminists need to ask "What exactly is the role of the Twelve Steps in women's recovery from alcoholism and how do women reconcile the Twelve Step program with their own feminist beliefs and behaviors?"

In any event, the Twelve Steps are part of a larger program of recovery that has been described as a mutual aid society and a fellowship (Alcoholics Anonymous 1952). The central organizational unit of AA is its small group meeting, where individuals with a desire to stop drinking learn about the Twelve Steps and build a sense of fellowship with and draw support from other AA members. The program is a collective effort, as one alcoholic helps another with their common disease. It is often heard in AA that, "we do together what we cannot do alone." While AA as an organization has had great success in its collective approach to arresting alcoholism and while AA is the premier model of how to promote recovery from alcoholism, it has been little studied, and the experience of recovering alcoholics in it— especially, it must be added, female alcoholics—remains improperly understood.

Obviously, if almost 700,000 women constituting more than one-third of AA's total membership have voluntarily joined AA, it must have something attractive and helpful to the alcoholic woman. At the same time, the environment of AA has posed problems for many women alcoholics. Although the only requirement for membership in AA is a desire to stop drinking, women have not always felt welcome in the rooms of AA. Negative stereotypes about alcoholic women prevailed at the time of AA's early development and continue to persist, even today. The social stigma, shame, and taboo of being a female alcoholic was so great that many women felt too inhibited to admit their alcoholism. It was thought that "nice" women didn't become drunks (Berenson 1991), and the cultural image of the "moral woman" (Hallberg 1988) was not easily extinguished by men or women inside AA, even though most AA members believed alcoholism was a physiological disease and not a problem of character. Moreover, as women began to share their stories inside AA, they perceived a double standard applied to them as alcoholic women. Also, some of the men and some of the wives of the alcoholics felt it was dangerous to include women in AA groups, where indiscrete relationships might develop. Although AA as an organization did not discriminate against women, the differing cultural expectations related to gender manifested themselves among some of the members of AA and among many women who might have needed the help that AA could offer. Consequently, it took several years for women's membership in AA to increase, and still today many American women feel that a double standard exists concerning women and alcoholism.

Despite initial cultural barriers to women's participation in AA, women's membership in AA has grown significantly. The first rise in women's membership occurred in the mid-1940s, owing to the advocacy efforts of Marty Mann, the first woman to join and maintain membership in AA. She joined AA in 1937, and by 1944 she was traveling around the United States on speaking tours encouraging women to seek help for alcoholism. The second upsurge in women's membership occurred in the late 1960s and early 1970s. At this time, the public awareness of alcoholism had grown, and many more people accepted the medical explanation that alcoholism was a disease that needed to be treated. Moreover, famous women had begun to speak out about alcoholism, which helped to educate the public about the disease of addiction.[5] Since 1968, the General Services Office (GSO) of AA has followed female membership trends, and records from the mid-1980s on consistently show that over a third of all AA members are women.

Women's participation in AA has increased not only due to the factors discussed above, but also due to the creation and growth of women-only groups. Women in AA noted that the Twelve Steps are written in a masculine voice and that the meeting milieu of AA reflects aspects of a patriarchal society. As a response to this, women in AA have created their own collective spaces by introducing the women-only AA meeting. Women-only meetings exclude men, but otherwise operate just like the other 'mixed' gender meetings of AA. The first "Women's Meeting for Alcoholics Only" was established in Cleveland, Ohio in 1941 (Vourakis 1989). The next group emerged in Minneapolis in 1942, and between 1945 and 1947 fourteen women-only groups started in fourteen different cities across the U.S. (Hallberg 1988). Today, women's groups can be found across the U.S. and world-wide.

Women-only meetings developed as a response to the uneasiness women felt in male-dominated AA meetings. The culture of the women's meetings differed from the regular meetings, because women brought with them styles and forms of expression not common among men. For example, in women-only meetings women tend to express their emotions, including crying, more freely. Moreover, because women tend to feel "safer" in women-only meetings, they disclose more intimate detail of their lives (Vourakis 1989). Women also feel more comfortable speaking about issues not directly related to their immediate concern of alcoholism. For example, women may talk about childhood abuse, sexual abuse or harassment, and other forms of assault. Similarly, women speak more candidly than men about their relationships with significant others and tend to focus on emotions more than men. Finally, women tend to discuss mental health issues, such as depression, more than men and focus more on building self-esteem, rather than deflating pride or ego, which are primary concerns for men in AA (Kaskutus 1992).

Although women's meetings offer an environment made for and by the women in AA, there is no strong evidence to suggest that women prefer women's meetings as compared to mixed meetings of AA. Rather, women attend different meetings where there are other women who appear to be concerned about the same recovery issues as themselves (Vourakis 1989). For example, in early recovery women are worried about staying sober, while in later recovery women are more concerned about other areas of personal growth in their lives. Seeking groups with women like themselves has sometimes meant women-only meetings, but this is not the central criterion on which women have based their choice of meeting attendance. Moreover, while some women prefer mixed groups, others who have not had previous exposure to positive female role models resist attending women-only groups. Additionally, for those women who have attended women-only groups, there has been no significant social or psychological characteristic common to these women (Vourakis 1989).

Related research also reflects inconclusive findings about how women feel about AA as an organization. It has been suggested that AA promotes a feminine ethic similar to that of the consciousness-raising groups of the second-wave feminist movement (Trevino 1990). Each may be characterized by few governing rules, lack of hierarchy, sharing of tasks among members, informal networking between groups, and rapid growth based on autonomous groups. Other attributes of the feminine ethic include emphases on self-disclosure, social-emotional behavior, conformity to group norms, cooperation, trust, equity, agreement, empathy, and anti-elitism (Trevino 1990). However, it has also been noted that not all feminists of the second-wave value this apparent feminine ethic. Rather, they seek to emulate masculine organizational traits such as instrumentality, competition, formal rules, hierarchy, and bureaucratization. These women view the feminine ethic of organizations like AA as:

> a distraction from the sexism entrenched in the culture of society. Their objective is the abolition of sexism through a restructuring of patriarchal culture. For the structural feminist, finding social satisfaction in the feminine ethic is simply a temporal crutch detrimental to their objective (Trevino 1990, 216).

It is this difference in feminist interpretation that helps to explain why organizations are not necessarily valued by all women uniformly and what is feminine may, or may not, be understood as feminist.

Whatever the precise nature of the experience in AA and in other twelve-step movements, one fact is undeniable—women's participation in and influence on the recovery movement has continued to grow. As mentioned above, in the early 1940s women initially met with resistance to joining the original twelve-step program of Alcoholics Anonymous, and their numbers were few. Today, women make up at least one-third of all AA membership throughout the world, and in some areas they constitute one half of AA membership (Mäkelä et al. 1996). Similarly, women's attendance at other chemical dependency programs has increased at a faster rate than that of men. Moreover, women have been more instrumental than men in creating new twelve-step programs that address non-chemical addictions such as love, sex, and relationship addictions. In fact, the expansion of the twelve-step model into other areas of living has been termed the "feminization" of recovery (Rapping 1996).

Feminist Interpretations of AA and the Study's Methodology

In broad outline, the feminist literature on women in AA reflects two diverging research interpretations. According to one feminist interpretation, women have been passive receptors of the AA philosophy and corresponding twelve-step culture (Faludi 1991; Bebko and Krestan 1991; Rapping 1996; Tallen 1995; Walters 1995). This view suggests that women are not aware of the patriarchal influences prevailing in AA or how these influences affect them. Feminists critical of AA point to the Twelve Steps as potentially dangerous to women, since they are perceived to be similar to traditional religious practices that are thought to be a part of the larger male ideological superstructure that is oppressive to women. Moreover, these feminists are anxious about the culture of the twelve-step movement and its spreading effects on the whole of society. For example, Elaine Rapping in *The Culture of Recovery* (1996) argues that the twelve-step model of AA has been adopted by the popular culture and generalized to many other social and psychological problems. As a consequence, it has been generalized to other so-called addictions, which has created, in her opinion, a generation of women who have become self-absorbed and interested only in personal development rather than in political achievements for women. Hence, feminist critics argue, the twelve-step movement and its culture are not just neutral and distracting, but rather are actively negative and detrimental, since they encourage women to view themselves as the problem rather than organizing to change the general socio-political environment. This contributes, in this reading of the situation, to a self-defeating orientation that sets the problem as personal, psychological, and internal rather than viewing the problem as political, sociological, and external.[6]

In contrast, the other feminist interpretation views women as active participants in developing a feminist culture within AA and the twelve-step movement (Davis 1997; Levi 1996; Van Den Bergh 1991; Schaef 1987). Feminist analysts of this school view AA and the twelve-step movement primarily as a therapeutic exercise, which has been very successful in helping women psychologically in terms of emotional and behavioral health. These therapists, psychologists, and educators integrate feminist principles into their work with women who attend twelve-step recovery programs and recommend that women modify the Twelve Steps to fit their own feminist interpretations. For example, Melody Beattie in *The Codependents Guide to the Twelve Steps* (1990) suggests that women completing the Fourth Step not only take an inventory of their character defects as instructed by the step, but also include a list of character assets at the same time.[7] Beattie recommends this, because women coming into AA or other twelve-step programs often have low self-esteem and do not need to emphasize excessively their negative characteristics. Similarly, for the Eighth Step, Beattie recommends that women not only make a list of those people they may have harmed by their addiction, but also make a list of those who have harmed them.[8] Again, Beattie suggests this, because she feels that women suffer from a lot of guilt, shame and remorse when they come into recovery. Beattie and others do not promote changing the Twelve Steps but merely recommend putting a gender lens on the interpretation and practice of the step.

Feminist researchers with a sympathetic orientation toward women's involvement in the twelve-step movement cite other aspects of women's experience as evidence that women can benefit from the variety of programs. As has been noted, many women who come into recovery have been the victims of physical, emotional, or sexual abuse or assault. Additionally, women still perceive that society has a harsher and more negative view of the woman alcoholic or addict than it does of her male counterpart. These feminists (i.e., Beattie and Shaef) assert that they are not promoting a victim mentality among women. Rather, they argue, women experience their addictions differently than men, and often this includes coming into recovery with many negative feelings and perceptions about one's self. They urge women to create a culture of recovery that they are more comfortable with, and they believe that, once in recovery, women have the opportunity to heal and empower themselves through the Twelve Steps.

The feminist interpretations just described have been categorized in a somewhat dichotomous fashion in order to allow for clarity in assessing the feminist literature about women in AA and the larger twelve-step movement. Not all feminists fall into either camp exclusively; however, the literature does tend to cluster around one of these two polar positions. This may be a consequence of leftover ideological differences between feminists of the second wave. The feminists that view the twelve-step culture as detrimental to feminism continue to view feminism as primarily a political movement. This is obvious in the criticisms Elaine Rapping levels against the culture of recovery. More subtle voices exist. For example, some literature criticizes AA as a movement that remains a largely white, middle-class self-help movement that does not accommodate women or diversity well. This critique has not been well studied, and little information is available on the experience of women of color in AA or of women not of the middle class. On the other hand, the feminists more favorable to the twelve-step movement concentrate more on the therapeutic aspects of the twelve-step movement and defend women's use of the support found in the movement. Less prominent are those voices, such as Denzin's in *The Recovering Alcoholic* (1987), that interpret alcoholism and the recovery process in AA as a unique experience. Denzin provides an interpretive framework from which to understand the state of being an alcoholic, but he has focused most of his work on the male alcoholic experience in AA rather than the female experience. He has, however, acknowledged the feminist debate, and he suggests that some women may indeed get stuck in the twelve-step recovery ideology, ever trying to change themselves to no avail, while other women more efficiently utilize the Twelve Steps to empower themselves (Denzin 1993).

Whatever the critics' interpretation, one generalized question underlies the literature about women in AA, and that is "What is the nature of empowerment among women in the twelve-step movement?" For those who prefer the political construct of feminist empowerment associated with second-wave feminism, empowerment is a collective outcome of women working together to better their social position. For those who are concerned about women's social-psychological development, empowerment is more of a personal construct. No matter how empowerment is framed and defined, both approaches assume a dialectical interaction between the sociological and psychological processes that ultimately end in a form of empowerment.

This research will address both types of empowerment–collective and individual–throughout the course of this study. The central argument throughout this work is that women empower themselves as members of AA and the larger twelve-step movement and they do so in a dynamic and interactive manner that is both sociological and psychological. This study will treat empowerment—as reflected in the lives and experiences of women in AA—as both a process and an outcome.

In order to understand women's struggle with their alcoholism and their victory in recovering from alcoholism, this research draws primarily on two schools of feminist thought—liberal feminism and phenomenological feminism. Together, these two perspectives provide an integrated analysis of women's experience of alcohol addiction and recovery. This approach demonstrates how women resist their addiction to alcohol and how they simultaneously empower themselves as a result of recovery from alcoholism. The first theoretical perspective, liberal feminism, supplies a collective framework for understanding empowerment. The second theoretical perspective, phenomenological feminism, provides an interpretive lens through which to view the experience of individual women as they resist alcoholism and recover from it. Hence, liberal feminism allows me to understand their collective experience as both women and alcoholics, while phenomenological feminism elucidates their subjective consciousness of both of those realities. The application of both theoretical approaches allows this study to augment measurable indicators of feminist empowerment with the subjective accounts of the alcoholic woman's experience.

The liberal-feminist critique of the twelve-step movement appears to be motivated by a real concern about how women are interpreting their private emotional problems. These feminists fear that, if women revert back to framing their personal problems in private terms only and do not critically look at their social environment, then a backlash in emotional terms will occur and soon after a political backlash will arise. Therefore, it is reasonable to question the relationship between the feminist movement and the twelve-step movement by asking women in AA about their gender-role attitudes, their views toward the feminist movement, their level of involvement in feminist activities, and whether or not they consider themselves feminist. That is, are the concerns of liberal feminists well placed and has there been a regression in feminist consciousness among women who have adopted the twelve-step program as a means to escape alcohol addiction? Or, alternatively, have these women been able to incorporate the elements of the twelve-step program without sacrificing liberal feminist political views? Or, even further, has the experience of personal recovery through the twelve-step program enhanced, extended, or intensified the liberal feminist convictions of these women?

In addition to looking at empowerment through the lens of second-wave feminists this research is informed by the feminist phenomenological theoretical tradition. A sociologist, C. Wright Mills, spoke of the necessity of understanding the inner life of the social actor and of connecting this account of the personal to the larger social structures (Mills 1959). Mills moved the social analysis of human behavior into a more reflexive discourse by looking at the relationship between subjective awareness and social structure. Alfred Schultz's (1972) work advanced Mill's sociological imagination in that he too advocated understanding social phenomena from the inter-subjectivity of the actor, while he simultaneously interprets his lived experience from the standpoint that he occupies—a standpoint that is defined by and limited to the social structure in which the individual lives. Although Alfred Schultz did not conceive of his phenomenological-sociological method as particularly feminist (Levesssue-Lopan 1988), feminist theorists (e.g., Belenky et al. 1986; Lorber and Farrell 1991; Reinharz 1983; and Smith 1978) have borrowed from Schultz's ideas about understanding social reality through the subjective experiences of social actors and have applied them to the study of women. Feminist theorists have readily turned to this phenomenological perspective, because it offers an alternative to positivistic scientific methodology, which studies women as objects rather than as subjects. Similarly, Schultz's focus on the mundane experiences making up the social world of actors has been of particular relevance to feminist scholars, since women have not historically held public positions or occupied social locations thought worthy of scientific understanding. Therefore, the focus on understanding women through their own subjective consciousness and their own lived reality, as it occurs in the everyday, has served the feminist scientific project well. Here, too, the personal tragedy of alcoholism among women can be well illustrated by asking the woman herself what it is like to be a female alcoholic. Subsequently, to allow her personal interpretation to inform the social scientific study of alcoholism among women ties her individual reality to the larger collective social problem of substance abuse in America. The current research project continues in this tradition and utilizes the phenomenological-sociological method to further define and describe twelve-step empowerment.

A unique mode of feminist analysis that is built upon the phenomenological tradition is what Dorothy Smith (1978) describes as the problematic of the everyday. According to Smith, the study of the ordinary facts of women's lives is where feminist analysis begins and all that women experience is worthy of scientific analysis and interpretation. The individual and her interpretation of reality is the unit of study. The researcher merely prompts the investigation into the everyday consciousness of women and allows them to tell their own stories. The key to this analytical project is to "get" what the woman as subject believes and not what the researcher studying the woman as object believes. In this way, feminist researchers find the "truth" of women's experiences.

In keeping with the feminist theoretical perspective, I employ a feminist methodology in order to examine how women empower themselves in the twelve-step program of Alcoholics Anonymous. Feminist methodology utilizes strict rules of empirical analysis while also allowing the motivations of the researcher to be stated. In some instances, feminist methodology encourages the researcher to be visible and not absent from the data collection process. Research in this context is not only for heuristic and academic purposes but is to inform social change and action. It is in this framework that this research has been conducted. A combination of qualitative and quantitative methodology is utilized in order to best present a holistic picture of women's experiences as active alcoholics and in recovery. A survey was specifically designed to question women who attend women-only meetings of AA about their lives before and during their participation in AA. Volunteers, solicited from the survey, were asked to provide a written story of what their lives have been like as both active and recovering alcoholics. This rich assortment of qualitative data has been used to supplement the survey findings. Review of the AA literature, observation from meeting attendance, and professional familiarity gained from having worked as a substance abuse counselor provides the background through which I interpret the data.

This research is based upon a non probability sample of women who attend women-only Alcoholics Anonymous meetings in a large metropolitan area. The sample frame consists of the women who attend women's AA meetings listed in the "Where & When," the AA directory of meetings in the metropolitan area. Twenty-six women-only meetings provided the data base for this research. One–hundred and sixty-seven women make up the final sample. Full consent was obtained and ethical standards were adhered to during the course of this research.

Chapters 2 through 7 (henceforth, the findings chapters) will describe data in detail and will analyze and discuss associations made between variables. The sample will be described in terms of demographics, past history, participation in AA, working the Twelve Steps of AA, indicators of spirituality, feminist consciousness, and self-esteem. In addition to quantitative measurements, all of the findings chapters incorporate narrative passages from those women who provided a written account of their experience. Also, I provide information throughout the text that was gathered from the field, as I observed women inside the women-only AA meetings. This information is presented at times to provide a context for analysis and at other times used to clarify the research findings.

The research setting is the women-only AA meeting. AA's primary organizational unit is the AA group. Sometimes referred to as the AA meeting, the purpose of all AA groups or meetings, as the AA preamble states, is for members to "share their experience, strength, and hope with each other that they may solve their common problem and help others to recover from alcoholism." (Alcoholics Anonymous 1962) There are various types of AA meetings—open to the pubic, closed (open only to those with an alcohol problem), general discussion where any topic relevant to alcoholism can be discussed, step meetings that focus specifically on the Twelve Steps, Big Book discussion meetings where literature from the main text of AA is studied, speakers' meetings where one or two individuals fill up the meeting hour with the telling of their story, and beginners meetings which focus only on the first three steps of AA. The general discussion meetings are the most common. This is the usual format of the women-only AA meeting.

The survey instrument was carefully designed to capture data elements that would be meaningful for public policy analysts, as well as for those who directly work with the female substance abuser. To this end, familiar survey questions were utilized and more specific "clinical" questions were asked. The survey instrument was constructed out of items taken from the U.S. Census (2000), the General Social Survey (Davis & Smith 2007), other studies (Kaskutus 1992; Vourakis 1989) and also from questions created specifically for this survey. In addition, there are composite questions derived from the American Society of Addiction Medicine's (2000) Addiction Severity Index, a clinical assessment tool, as well as questions that model those found in epidemiological studies measuring alcohol dependency, abuse, and addiction.

The quantitative and qualitative data collected by the survey instrument are presented in the findings chapters.[9] In Chapter 2, I describe this sample of women in AA and compare it to a generalized profile of the female alcoholic. Additionally, the past history of this sample of women is presented, as well as the problems these women have encountered as active alcoholics. Chapter 2 also includes survey findings specific to the incidence of past physical or sexual abuse, women's family histories of alcoholism and addiction, and problems that have resulted as a consequence of alcoholic drinking. Next, Chapter 3 examines the level of involvement this sample of women have in AA and the larger twelve-step movement. This chapter clarifies the extent to which women are active agents in their own recovery and how they have shaped the culture of AA to fit their gendered needs. Focusing more specifically on the Twelve Steps of AA, Chapters 4, 5, and 6 analyze how women empower themselves through the process of working the Twelve Steps. Chapter 4, "Women's Struggle with Surrender," explores their experiences with the first three steps of AA. Chapter 5 examines how women clean up the "wreckage of their past" by working Steps Four through Nine. Chapter 6 illustrates how, by working the last three steps of AA, women develop and pass on the recovery they have experienced. This chapter also includes an analysis of how religion and spirituality are viewed and practiced among women in AA. These three chapters illuminate how women simultaneously practice resistance and acceptance of their alcoholism in light of a program based on spiritual principles.

Linking the Twelve Steps to women's empowerment, the concluding chapter "Empowering Women, Collectively and Individually" provides both an empirical analysis of feminist indices to reflect second-wave feminist conceptions of empowerment and narrative data that highlight more subjective recall of "other good things" or positive consequences women have experienced as a result of their sobriety in AA. Specifically, gender role attitudes, feminist beliefs, and feminist behaviors are measured and compared to another, broader sample of women taken from the General Social Survey (GSS). By combining quantitative measures of feminism and qualitative narrative data, this book concludes with a summary of the significant findings that reflect how women in AA empower themselves through both collective and individual means.

Notes

[1] In terms of membership and groups, Women for Sobriety is minuscule compared to AA. Its website at http://www.womenforsobriety.org/ contains no estimate of membership figures, but claims to have over 300 groups in seven countries.

---

[2] Second-wave feminism is that associated with the American and European feminist movement most active in the 1970's. This movement was characterized as fighting for equality between the sexes and other civil rights pertaining to women as a group.

[3] See the Alcoholics Anonymous website at http://www.alcoholics-anonymous.org/.

[4]The most explicit and condensed discussion of the spiritual experience is contained in Appendix II of *Alcoholics Anonymous*. There it is stated that an "awareness of a Power greater than ourselves is the essence of spiritual experience."

[5] The best-known example is that of Betty Ford, wife of President Gerald Ford, who publicized her problem with alcohol and became very involved in educating the nation about alcoholism. Mrs. Ford spoke out about the need to treat alcoholism as a disease, and she created her own treatment facility–the Betty Ford Clinic.

[6] This same view is expressed in the popularly-oriented account of women and alcoholism by Devon Jersild, *Happy Hours* (2001).

[7] The fourth step of AA reads "Made a searching and fearless moral inventory of ourselves."

[8]The eighth step of AA reads "Made a list of all persons we had harmed, and became willing to make amends to them all."

[9] This particular survey of women in AA was conducted and data collected in 2001. Three other data sources were also employed. They are the U.S. Census, The General Social Survey (GSS), and AA's 2004 Membership Survey.

2
Women and Alcoholism

Before turning to the experience of women alcoholics in AA, we need a clearer picture of who women alcoholics are and what factors contribute to their alcoholism. This chapter describes the demographic profile of this sample of female alcoholics and the nature of the problems these women have experienced that are directly related to their alcoholism. The demographic profile is discussed in the context of a broader literature review and compares this sample to women in the general public. Once the demographic picture has been outlined, attention shifts to the past abuse and other emotionally painful problems that these women have experienced that are connected in some way with their alcoholism.

It is necessary to understand who the female alcoholic is, as defined by general demographic information, before analyzing the particular experiences of women in AA. For decades, such a demographically-based picture of the woman alcoholic could not be sketched in, because drinking was thought of as a male activity. As was argued in the previous chapter, an associated and even more deeply rooted societal prejudice was the idea that heavy or alcoholic drinking was primarily a man's problem. As a result, most research on alcoholism concentrated on the study of males only. Over the past twenty years, however, women's use and abuse of alcohol has been more widely documented. There now exists an expanding, albeit still somewhat limited, base of empirical data in which an examination of how gender affects drinking behavior can be situated and to which new findings can be compared.

The second section in this chapter will discuss the past history of women whose lives have been scarred by the ravages of alcoholism. The questions in the survey on which this discussion will be based were formulated to address the problems that women experienced that led them to drink alcoholically, as well as the difficulties resulting from that drinking. The research literature on women alcoholics shows that they experience many different types of problems before they seek help for their alcoholism. Many have life histories filled with difficult—indeed, often devastating—experiences. A sense of the traumatic personal stories of many women alcoholics is essential background for understanding the gendered recovery they have shaped in AA.

General Demographics

As was mentioned above, there is a growing body of literature on alcoholism that takes into account how gender is related to drinking patterns and alcoholic behavior, and it also includes other demographic characteristics as part of the research into the ways that women drink. The expanded list of demographic variables now associated with women's drinking includes age, marital status, employment status, occupation, personal income, household income, educational attainment, race and ethnicity. These variables are employed in the following discussion of how women drink as essential background information for the analysis of the experiences and attitudes of the women alcoholics examined in this study. In social scientific analysis, drinking is typically discussed in terms of rates of alcohol consumption, number of problems related to drinking, and other indicators of alcohol dependence as defined by the American Psychiatric Association's *Diagnostic and Statistical Manual of Mental Disorders* (1994). In the context of this background summary, the most important issue is the relationship between various demographic variables and heavy, problem, or dependency drinking among women.

Gender

The gender gap between women and men's drinking in America is closing. In 2000, the National Household Survey on Drug Abuse found that 40.2 percent of all women in the United States drink and 53.6 percent of all men in the U.S. drink (National Institute on Drug Abuse, 2000). Moreover, the way in which women drink today is more like men's drinking. Not only do more women drink today than before, but they also consume more alcohol per drinking episode and have begun to experience just as many problems related to alcoholic drinking as do men. In 1982, women who drank consumed less alcohol than men and had fewer problems directly associated with alcohol abuse and fewer symptoms of dependency than did men (Malin, Coakley, and Kaelber 1982). Today, there is growing evidence that women drink more heavily and consequently develop drinking-related problems similar to men. Most striking is the fact that those women who become dependent on alcohol, report more problems and more severity in problems related to alcoholism than do male heavy drinkers (National Institute on Alcohol

Abuse and Alcoholism 1992). Therefore, not only are women beginning to drink more like men in terms of numbers who drink and how much is consumed, but also women are experiencing just as many or more problems associated with heavy and problem drinking as men. Unfortunately, in terms of women's drinking, closing the gender gap is not necessarily beneficial to women and in fact is most detrimental for those women who are alcoholics.

Age

To better plot the life histories of the alcoholic women surveyed in this study, age is another important factor. Age is a strong indicator of drinking behavior. Longitudinal surveys, such as the National Longitudinal Alcohol Epidemiology Survey (NLAES) sponsored by the National Institute on Alcohol Abuse and Alcoholism in 1992, and other epidemiological surveys have found age to be associated both with levels of alcohol consumption and with the style of drinking, as well as with alcohol dependence. In general, younger women (18-34 years of age) report higher rates of drinking-related problems than do older women (Hilton 1988; Wilsnack, Wilsnack, and Klassen 1984), while the incidence of alcohol dependence is greater among middle-aged women (35-49 years of age) than among younger or older women (Harford, Hanna, and Faden 1994). These findings support the disease model of alcoholism, which defines alcoholism as a progressive disease that develops over the time period that the substance is used. Although for cultural reasons younger adult women drink heavily, it is not until they are middle-aged that they become dependent on alcohol. Again, physiological and psychological dependency is a different and more severe form of drinking than heavy drinking, although heavy drinking can be very problematic.

The findings on age among the women in this sample correspond with the findings just cited. The average age of women in this study's sample is forty-eight years, and this is consistent with AA's 2004 Membership Survey that reflects a similar statistic.[1] In both this sample and AA as a whole, there are fewer members in the youngest and oldest age categories, and the most members are between the ages of thirty-one to sixty years old (see table 2.1).

Given the mean and the modal age of women in this sample, most of the women surveyed in this sample either experienced the 1960s-1970s women's movement first hand or came of age just following the peak of the second-wave feminist movement in the U.S. Only 21 percent of the women sampled, those over age sixty-one, came of age before the late

1960s. Therefore, most of the women making up this sample were likely to have had at least some exposure to and awareness of the feminist movement.

Marital Status

In addition to age, marital status is also significantly related to how women drink. Widowed women have the lowest rates of drinking, and married women have intermediate rates of drinking (Wilsnack et al.1994). Those women who have never been married or who are divorced or separated have the highest rates of heavy drinking and drinking-related problems. Not surprisingly, 40 percent of this sample have either never been married or are currently separated or divorced. Conversely, only 5 percent of the women in this sample report their spouse as deceased. This confirms what the AA membership survey reflects as well as other studies that show widowers are least likely to drink heavily or to be alcoholic.

Previous research findings linking marital status and alcoholism are further supported by comparing women in this sample of AA to women from the general population. For example, women in this AA sample are less likely to be married than women in the general population and almost twice as likely to be divorced or separated. Similarly, this sample of women in AA included half as many widowed women (5 percent) as does the sample from the March 2000 Census which is 10 percent. Not surprisingly, it can be argued that alcoholic drinking has a very negative impact on family and marriage stability (see table 2.1).

Employment Status & Occupation

Another demographic factor that has been linked to how women drink is employment status. Longitudinal studies have shown that employed women have higher rates of drinking than women who are not employed. However, heavy or problem drinking is similar between the two groups (Wilsnack et al.1994). Moreover, there is a growing body of literature that suggests that women with multiple roles such as marriage, family, and paid employment—women who, because of the extensive demands on their attention, time and energy, were sometimes called "Super Women" in the 1970s and 1980s—have reduced risks of both mental health and drinking problems (Fromberg, Gjerdingen and Preston 1986). Conversely, absence of multiple roles or the loss of roles for

Table 2.1 Summary of demographic variables that describe women in AA, the AA Membership Survey, & the U.S. Census (percent)

Variable/Value	Women in AA	AA Mem-bership	Census
Age			
Under 30	7	9.4	----
31-60 years	72	74.3	----
Over 60	21	16.3	----
Total N	(167)	(7,500)	----
Marital Status			
Married	44	38	52.3
Divorced/Separated	23	29	12.6
Never Married	21	29	25.1
Live with Mate	7	----	----
Widowed	5	4	10.0
Total N	(167)	(7,500)	(110,660)
Occupation			
Professional/technical	51	----	21.6
Manager/administrator	29	----	14.1
All Other Occupations	20		64.7
Total N	(167)	----	(63,102)
Personal Income			
Less than $20,000	21	----	30.9
$20,000–$49,999	45	----	56.1
$50,000–$74,999	14	----	9.3
$75,000 and over	20	----	3.7
Total N	(152)	----	(40,404)
Education			
Less than high school	3.0	----	17.3
High school graduate	8.4	----	37.0
Some college	8.6	----	28.2
College Graduate	70.0	----	17.5
Total N	(167)	----	(91,620)

Source: AA's 2004 Membership Survey & The March Supplement of the 2000 Census (United States Census Bureau 2000 a, b, c & d). Note: "Live with mate," under Marital Status was not a category provided by either the AA or the Census survey. AA's survey includes both men and women and does not provide information about personal income or education. Please see Alcoholics Anonymous (2004) for occupational status of AA members. The Census data includes only women.

women is related to heavy drinking (Wilsnack and Cheloha 1987). Type of employment has also been linked to how women drink. Studies have shown that nontraditional employment for women is linked to higher rates of drinking. This includes women in high-ranking executive positions and women employed in occupations where more than 50 percent of the workers are male (La Rosa 1990). Data indicates, then, that women who are strenuously engaged with diverse responsibilities are less likely to drink to excess, unless those responsibilities involve nontraditional employment.

Indeed, the majority of women in this sample, 63 percent, are employed in high status, male dominated occupations. For example, over half are employed in a professional or technical position and another 29 percent are managers or administrators. Also, one woman is in the military. Moreover, even for those women employed in occupations dominated by women, very few, ten, report performing traditionally women's work such as clerical, sales, or service. Overwhelmingly, the women in this particular sample are employed in fields that require education, training, or leadership abilities, all characteristics once associated with exclusively "male" occupations and those that have been found to be associated with heavy drinking.

Compared to the data on working women in the general American population, the women in this research are indeed over represented in higher status positions. In fact, an inverted pyramid may illustrate the comparison between the two groups by occupational titles held. Where this AA sample of women is top heavy in higher status, male dominated positions, American women, in general, are still over represented in lower status, female dominated occupations. According to a supplemental report to the 2000 Census, one-fifth of the American female work force is employed in professional or technical fields and just over 14 percent is employed in administrative or managerial positions. The majority occupy lower status positions (US Census Bureau 2000a). It is clear that this sample of women in AA is over represented in professional and managerial occupations compared to employed women from the general population (see table 2.1).

Personal & Household Income

Nine out of ten women in this sample claim a personal income. Of this group, three-fourths enjoy a personal income over $20,000. More striking, however, is that one-third earn an income over $50,000. Matched with the income of a spouse or partner, 90 percent of this sample reported income over $50,000 of which one-half claim $100,000 or more in household income. Without a doubt, this is an affluent sample of women in AA.

Compared to women from the general population, the women in this study's sample are significantly better off in terms of personal income. The percentages in the low and middle income categories are lower, and those in the top two earning categories are substantially higher. That is, there are fewer women at the bottom of the earning's ladder and more women at the top. Again, an inverted pyramid illustrates the difference between the two groups (see table 2.1).

Education

The women in AA surveyed for this study are well educated compared to women from the general population. According to the data from the 2000 Census, far more women in the general population have less than a high school degree and significantly fewer women are college graduates compared to the women surveyed for this study. For example, just over 17 percent of the women from the general population have less than a high school degree, while only 3 percent of the AA sample has less than a high school diploma or equivalent. Similarly, 17.5 percent of women in the general population are college graduates, while 70 percent of the women from this study's sample are college graduates. In sum, the women in this sample are over represented in higher levels of education compared to their counterparts in the general population. This high level of educational attainment helps to explain both the high percentage of women in high status employment occupations and the high personal earnings for the women in this sample.

Race/Ethnicity

There are discernible differences in the drinking habits of women compared across racial and ethnic groups in America. Of the three largest ethnic groups, white women are most likely to drink, African-American women are least likely to drink, and Hispanic women fall somewhere between the other two in terms of drinking (Catenao 1994). As expected, this sample consisted of a majority of white women, 87 percent of the sample, and the only other predominant racial group, African American, made up 9 percent of this sample. These findings are consistent with AA's membership survey which reflects 89 percent of the membership in the United States and Canada as white and just over 3 percent of the membership as black. [1]

Past History

The past experience of women who become alcoholics falls naturally into two parts. As a result, the questions for this study's survey address both the problems that contributed to the development of alcoholic drinking and the problems created by addictive drinking. The first set of questions relates to the problems that tend to precede the onset of alcoholism among women. These problems usually relate to past emotional, physical, or sexual abuse. The second category of questions asks women to what extent alcoholism and other drug addiction runs in their families. Most researchers and clinicians in the alcohol and drug addiction field believe that alcoholism is a family problem that results from both genetic predisposition and environmental influences. The third category of problems addressed in this section involves difficulties that generally co-exist with or result from abusive or addictive drinking. These problems include social, emotional, physical, and job-related difficulties. Often used as indicators of heavy drinking, problems such as the breakup of a marriage, loss of a job and poor health are examples of the consequences of addictive drinking. Also, dual addiction, defined as being addicted to more than one substance, is becoming increasingly prevalent among alcoholic women. This section will provide both quantitative and qualitative responses to questions that address each of these problem areas common to alcoholic women.

Past Abuse

Previous research has shown that many female alcoholics have been physically or sexually abused in their past (Covington 1982; Langeland and Hangers 1998; Murphy et al. 1980; and Wilsnack et al. 1994). Many have been victims of childhood abuse, and others have experienced abuse or assault as teenagers and adults. Some have suffered multiple forms of abuse, and some women have experienced abuse both as children and as adults. Consequently, there appears to be a strong association between a history of sexual abuse and alcohol addiction. It was expected, then, that this study would reveal that a significant proportion of its sample had a history of abuse or assault.

Not surprisingly, the numbers and chronic nature of abuse in this sample is a violent story to tell. Out of 167 women surveyed, 60 percent have either been physically or sexually assaulted (includes abused) in their past. More alarming, however, is that one-fifth report they were victims of childhood incest. In addition to the large numbers who have been abused, the persistent nature of abuse is seen, too. Close to 20 percent of these women have been both physically and sexually assaulted in the past. Representing the worse cases, almost 13 percent have not only experienced both physical and sexual assault, but have also been victims of childhood incest. These findings suggest a pattern of chronic violation, including child abuse, during which the same individual is subjected to multiple and severe forms of abuse. Moreover, much of the abuse these women have experienced is not at the hands of a stranger, but occurs in or near their own homes and involves family members or friends. These data correspond to previous research that has found alcoholic women are more likely than not to have histories of childhood sexual abuse including incest (Covington 1982; Peluso and Peluso 1988). Like other samples of women who abuse alcohol or drugs, this sample too reveals a pattern of abuse that occurs prior to a woman's maturity and often before her active alcohol addiction. Therefore, victimization in childhood is often a significant antecedent to alcohol and other substance abuse among women (see table 2.2).

One explanation for this relationship is that women begin to drink to escape the pain and memories associated with childhood abuse. If not immediately, then as the girl grows into a woman, she finds that alcohol or other mood-altering substances allow her to hide from her sexuality or to "act out" in sexual ways. In either case, the woman uses alcohol to facilitate entry into adult sexuality, a sexuality with which she is not comfortable or for which she is not emotionally ready. One woman made the connection herself between her past experience of sexual violation and later sexual conduct, while writing her personal history for this research project. She writes:

> I was sexually molested in a movie theater once when I was about 6 years old. It was a terrifying experience which I "forgot" and buried for years, remembering it only around about the time I got into treatment. After the violation, I experimented with sex with older boys and now realize the connection that the sexual molestation led to my precociously acting out sexually at an early age.

Another example of how past abuse thwarts a women's developing sexuality is well illustrated in the following excerpt from a respondent's story:

> The spring before my 16th birthday I was raped and this became a repeated rape throughout the whole long summer. This experience had damaging effects. I developed coping mechanisms and learned to bury the experience. I lied because I was scared to tell the truth. I felt responsible, like it was my fault.

The following is also an excerpt from a respondent's story that describes how she was a victim of incest and how this affected her family relations.

> I was never close to my mother, but I was a "daddy's girl" until puberty. I have blocked out much of my childhood, and realize that this was in large part because my father engaged in some sexual activity with me between the ages of five and ten. My father would tell me that we needed to be close because my mother was frigid. This abnormal relationship naturally encouraged a jealousy and competition between me and my mother. Until her death, my mother denied knowing anything about the activities between me and my father and today I realize that this may be true. But I drank at my feelings of guilt, shame, resentment and anger at my mother for not intervening for many years.

The personal accounts of women's past abuse point directly to why some women begin to drink and ultimately become alcoholic. The personal stories also describe the emotional obstacles women need to overcome in getting sober from alcohol. Given that victims of childhood abuse and sexual assault often blame themselves, issue of self-esteem are great (Katz 1991; Kirpatrick 1986; and Koss et al. 1988), and psychological despair, heightened and further complicated when abuse is at the hands not of a complete stranger but by someone they knew and trusted (Fox and Gilbert 1994).

Family Addiction

It is widely thought that alcoholism is a family disease that is shared within and across generations. In 1977 the National Institute on Alcohol Abuse and Alcoholism (NIAAA) reported that first-degree relatives of alcoholics are two to seven times more likely to become alcohol dependent than people with nonalcoholic relatives. Additionally, after analyzing data from the 1992 National Longitudinal Alcohol Epidemiologic Survey, NIAAA concluded in 1998 that a family history of alcoholism has a substantial effect on the development of alcohol dependency over the life span. NIAAA does not attempt to explain why this association exists. However, research on alcoholism tends to follow in one of two traditions—a genetic and biological approach or a structural and environmental one. The association between alcoholism and family history can be explained from either perspective, and often research integrates the two perspectives when studying familial effects of alcoholism.

Table 2.2 Summary of the problems experienced by women in AA
(percent)

Variable/Value	Women in AA
Abuse	
Physical Abuse	32.0
Sexual Abuse	29.9
Incest	20.0
Physical/Sexual Abuse	18.9
Physical/Sexual/Incest	13.0
Addiction in the Family	
Father	50.6
Sister/Brother	51.2
Grandparents	36.1
Mother	30.9
Husband/Mate	30.7
Own Children	13.0
Other relatives	26.5
Other Problems	
Depression	77.2
Social Embarrassment	71.3
Suicidal Thoughts	55.1
Violent Behavior	30.5
Car Accidents	29.3
Divorce/separation	25.1
Other Drug Abuse	
Cocaine	22.3
Barbiturates/Prescription drugs	14.9
Marijuana	13.6
Crank/Speed/Hallucinogens	13.0
Heroin/Methadone	4.3
Total N	(167)

Note: Respondents not limited to one response only.

Regardless of the cause, this study revealed a very strong connection between alcohol and drug abuse in the family of origin or among those who raised these women. Over half of this sample report having been raised by an alcoholic parent. The numbers are higher (upwards of 80 percent) when identifying alcoholic or drug abusing parents irrespective of who raised them. While these women vary in their interpretations of nature versus nurture, the desire to escape the dynamics of the alcoholic home is similar to the woman who has been physically or sexually abused. Moreover, these women work not only to escape the dysfunction of the families they were raised in but also attempt to avoid becoming alcoholic parents themselves. However, in spite of their best intentions, they too recreate the cycle of dependence and potential dysfunction. As one woman puts it:

> Both my mother and father always drank too much. The beer man came on Thursdays (payday) and delivered two cases of quarts and they were gone long before the next Thursday. My parents would sit up and drink late into the night and got uglier and uglier toward each other with each sip. Many nights their arguing and fighting made me and my siblings crawl into bed together and wish real hard that we were somewhere else. My parents actually fought everyday for the forty-four years they were married before my Dad died. His life was miserable. I now know that he was depressed and that coupled with his drinking made him no fun to be around. The fact that my mother belittled him unmercifully didn't help. I never wanted to be like him and I have tried hard not to be even though I have all the same DNA—bipolar, diabetes, high blood pressure etc. and my mother spent years telling me how I was just like him. That is a bad tape I have worked hard to erase.

In addition to having alcoholic parents, over half of this sample report that they have siblings who are alcoholics or drug abusers. The survey does not differentiate between a sibling or siblings who suffer from active alcoholism and those who no longer drink. Sometimes AA members have siblings who are not alcoholics themselves. Others have siblings who still drink alcoholically, and others still have siblings in recovery. In many cases, it is a mixture of scenarios. One woman noted in her narrative account that:

> Many studies have been done trying to find out if there is a genetic factor in alcoholism. My family of origin is composed of five siblings—three boys and two girls. We are all alcoholics although there was no drinking in our home. My older brother died sober (3 years) of cancer in 1992 at 65 years of age. My younger brother died in 1975 of alcoholic cirrhosis of the liver (2 years sober). My sister 67 years old still drinks and my youngest brother 66 years old is now sober 8 years. My daughter has 15 years of sobriety.

With over 50 percent of this sample's participants indicating that they have alcoholic or drug addicted siblings, it seems safe to call addictive behavior "a family affair."

In addition to alcoholic parents and siblings, respondents also report that one-third of them have grandparents who were alcoholic, and one-fourth of the women report having cousins, aunts and uncles who are alcoholic or drug addicts. Moreover, in addition to blood relatives, over 30 percent of the women in this sample have husbands who are alcoholic (see table 2.2). Remarkably, the only aspect of family life that does not appear to be overwhelmed by alcoholism or other addictions is in the offspring of these women. That only 23 percent of those who are mothers in this sample report having children who are alcoholic or drug addicts is a hopeful finding. This statistic suggests that the rate of alcoholism and addiction can be reduced between generations. However, it is also clear in this sample that, if alcoholism is found among both parents, the rate of substance abuse on the part of the child increases.[2]

It is not clear what role membership in AA plays in decreasing the rate of addictions found between generations. However, we do know from the qualitative data collected, that an alcoholic parent who gets sober in AA has the opportunity to act as a role model for their own children. This does not mean that a child of a parent in AA will not become an addict herself; it simply means that there is an awareness that one can recover from alcoholism or other addictions. For example, one woman revealed that, "I broke the cycle of hopelessness in reference to alcoholism running in the family. I showed by example how AA and a new way of life work. My son has been in recovery 1 year and my husband is trying but struggling." Another respondent provided a diagram of a family tree tracking the alcoholism in her family, and she summarizes the extent of alcoholism in the present generation "My mom is the grandparent of six men. Three of those young men (ages 16-40) have had early rehabs and AA/NA and two continue to use but they are aware that help is out there." This woman, in recovery herself, remarks that she uses a family tree as a way to point out the genetic predisposition to alcoholism and to educate others in how to break the family cycle.

It is not clear what the negative effects are upon the children of the alcoholic women in this survey, but, again through qualitative data, the women in this sample have provided some insight into what their own experiences were as children of alcoholics. Both the effects of growing up with an alcoholic parent and the promise of recovery in AA are well illustrated in the following narratives provided by respondents in this sample. One woman writes:

I was (and still am) very emotional and grew up worshiping an alcoholic father who could not stay sober, no matter how many times he was whisked away in an ambulance to the Veteran's hospital to dry out. He couldn't stay sober until he finally joined Alcoholic's Anonymous. By that time, I was 25 and deeply immersed in a secret world of my own drugs and drinking. He stayed sober the last ten years of his life, thanks to AA. His experience helped me to believe when I decided to join that if AA worked for him, it could certainly work for me.

Another woman writes:

AA was familiar to me because my father had been in AA in the mid-1950s, when I was a teenager. The whole family used to go to open speaker meetings. I don't think I had thought about AA for 20 years. I went back to the same meeting that my father used to go to. My uncle was just starting back into the program at this time, January 1979, and we went to meetings together for a while.

Given the entanglement between women and their families, it is expected that the relationships between women and empowerment will vary given the extent of alcoholism that is in the family. Previous research demonstrates that childhood adversity related to alcoholism and violence in the home leads to depression and other long-term effects on adults (Deming, Chase, and Karesh 1996). Moreover, alcoholic families tend to express more anger, exhibit more negative messages among family members, show less warmth, cohesion, and direct communication than nonalcoholic families (Garbarino and Strange 1993; Senchak et al. 1995). Members of alcoholic families tend to be more prone to anxiety, depression and stress-related disorders than members of nonalcoholic families. Adult children of alcoholics, especially, are more likely to have less fulfilling lives as demonstrated by less satisfaction in their family relations with their spouses and children (Kerr and Hill 1992; Hall, Bolen, and Webster 1994). Similarly, adult children of alcoholics tend to have dependency needs on others that harm their adult relations (Lyon and Greenberg 1991).

Other Related Problems

Women suffering from alcoholism experience many different types of problems as a direct result of their addiction. Often women experience multiple difficulties before they seek treatment. Sometimes a particular problem becomes a turning point for the woman, and she realizes she needs help. In other instances, outside authorities intervene and refer the woman to treatment or AA. Whatever the course, experiencing difficulties related to drinking indicates at the very least problem drinking and at its worst alcoholic drinking.

Women alcoholics experience many social, psychological, and health care problems. One problem that was expected to appear in these alcoholic women's lives is depression. Yet, despite the fact that depression is a well-founded accompaniment of alcoholism, its affect and pervasiveness were nonetheless remarkable.

Depression

Over three quarters of these women, answered "yes" to depression as a problem associated with their drinking. This finding is consistent with other research linking depression and alcoholism in women. Depression can be both an antecedent to alcoholism and can co-occur with alcoholism. However, some clinical research indicates that depression tends to exist before the development of alcoholism among women. For example, one study found that of the women examined in the Epidemiologic Catchment Area Study (Hezler, Burham, and Keener 1991) who had co-occurring depression and alcoholism, depression preceded drinking problems in 66 percent.[3] A respondent in this present study illustrates well the way in which alcoholism followed the battle she fought late in her life with depression. She describes it, as follows:

> Always in life, I have held myself completely responsible for my actions and so I honestly cannot blame anyone else for my failings. On my forty-ninth birthday, I felt that I could not continue with this life of shame and humiliation and so I said goodbye to my boyfriend. At about the same time I was given an early retirement from my job and I also became physically ill. I became so depressed and despondent that I began drinking very, very heavily. Most days I was in a stupor. I drank and slept until I could drink again. At no time during my journey did I ever deny that I was an alcoholic, but there didn't seem to be any help for me. I could go for thirty days without drinking, but in reality, I was only counting off the days until I could drink again. Mercifully for me, in April of 1991 my family decided to do an intervention and have nothing further to do with me while I was still drinking. No one bothered to tell me about this and I only assumed that everyone on this earth had deserted me. I could never relate to anyone the bottomless pit that I existed in for the next several months.

Suicidal Thoughts

Related to both alcoholism and depression is suicidal thinking. Over half of these women reported that they have had suicidal thoughts. Having such thoughts is common among women suffering from alcoholism (Hill 1984). Sometimes, the thinking is subtle and is reflected in simply not having the desire to live or to fight the addiction, any longer. Some women equate symptoms of depression, such as not wanting to get out of bed and long periods of isolation, with feelings of not wanting to live. Other women believe they do not have the right to live due to their own remorse and guilt about their alcoholism. Also, women who do act on their suicidal thoughts tend to use means that do not result in fatality, whereas men tend to use means such as guns that are more effective and definitive. Similarly, women who "act out" their suicidal thoughts often are "asking" for help and, if fortunate, get the help they need. For other women, it can be a turning point in their addiction, because they end up seeking help for their addiction after they have reached the critical stage of acting out a suicidal thought.

Mental illness

In addition to depression, other mental illness tends to co-occur with alcoholism (Bryer et. al. 1987; Bucholz 1992). Labeled as dually-diagnosed, women with an accompanying mental illness have an even harder time getting and staying sober. Often their mental illness is masked by the use of alcohol, and for some using alcohol is a form of self-medicating. More damaging, however, is the denial that accompanies both the disease of alcoholism and other forms of mental illness. The following excerpt is from a respondent's story, which details the misery that comes with being dually-diagnosed. She writes:

> At about the age 11 years, I began to experience symptoms of the Obsessive Compulsive Disorder (OCD)—the countless (4-6 per day) hot-hot baths, checking the stove, checking the light switches over and over again before going out, and thinking that I might be seeing things (bacteria) in the air that no one else could see. Then, at about 15 years, I began to experience symptoms of depression. I experimented with sex (even though I was sexually dysfunctional then and continue to be asexual today), got pregnant, and cut my wrist, which landed me in my first psychiatric hospital stay for 5 months. I had electric shock treatment and an abortion. I went back to high school, finished with honors and went away to college on scholarship. Neither my mother nor our family said nothing [sic], no explanation for what had happened to me, why it might have happened, nothing. Actually,

several knew or suspected something about my natural father, which they did not divulge until I confronted them and demanded information at the request of my psychiatrist about the time I went into rehab.

Stigma

After depression, the next most frequent problem listed was social embarrassment. Over 70 percent of the sample reported "yes," they had suffered social embarrassment as a result of their drinking. This is an expected result given the feelings of shame women have as alcoholics. Social stigmas and stereotypes of the female alcoholic increase a woman's sense of embarrassment, as she becomes a problem drinker. One respondent offers her own reflection on how stigmas and stereotypes affected her own image of what an alcoholic is:

> I may have been more open to help earlier if it were not that to me the alcoholic was the wino in the street. It was okay for a man to drink too much but not a woman, for she was seen as a slut, low life, bad mother, bad wife, etc. In my view AA, composed mostly of men, was for those who had no self control, were not educated, came from very bad home lives, had lost their families and possessions and were basically the dregs of the earth. I being educated, white, upper middle class female, with a husband, children, house and a job definitely did not belong in AA or in counseling for alcohol. Of course, I also knew that if I admitted to anyone I was alcoholic, I would have to stop drinking and that was not an option. In short, I believe that my view of alcoholics and AA are that of the general public, which is extremely uneducated as to the disease and stigmatizes anyone, especially women, who drink excessively to the point of destroying their lives and those around them. It is this general ignorance that plays a major role in preventing people, in particular women, from getting help when they need it.

Also related to and often the result of social embarrassment is the loss of friends. Almost half reported that they had lost friends as a result of their drinking. Alcoholic women pay a heavy price for their addiction.

Health

Another unfortunate side-effect of heavy drinking is health problems. The majority of these women report having not taken care of their physical health as a result of their drinking. The women in this sample are well educated and have fairly high levels of income. The problem of lack of information about and access to health care, which has been discussed in connection with the poor health of minority women and women from lower economic categories, is not the problem for this group of women. However, almost one-half of these women identified poor health care as a problem associated to drinking. This suggests that women in the throes of addiction often do not care for themselves as they should, even when they have the means to do so. In addition, the impetus to deny the existence or the severity of their alcoholism and the stigma or shame of being labeled an alcoholic deters women from seeking health care. Further complicating the picture is the fact that many women in this sample also report having co-addictions to other drugs and substances. These findings suggest that alcoholic women—no matter how informed or economically well off—will have problems connected with poor health care (see table 2.2).

Violence, Dangerous Driving, and the Shame of Arrest

The following three problems (violence, car accidents and arrests) typically associated with male drinking behavior are now characteristic of women's drinking. Approximately 30 percent of these women admit to having a problem with violent behavior or getting into car accidents due to drinking. Over a fifth of the sample reported having been arrested due to drinking. For problem drinkers, arrests typically mean a driving under the influence (DUI) or driving while intoxicated (DWI) charge. Although this survey does not differentiate between drunk driving and other crimes, the following remark from a respondent illustrates well the chronic and multiple incidences of problems related to drinking and driving. She states "Again, within a month I received my third DWI. I had finally reached my bottom. This time I had totaled my car, and spent 24 hours in the county detention center." A second woman describes the end of her drinking and states, "I got my fourth (and hopefully last) DWI, just a few blocks from my house." Violence, dangerous and illegal driving, and the shame of arrest are surprisingly common (see table 2.2).

Divorce/Separation

Yet another outcome of alcoholic drinking that is common for men and is becoming increasingly common for women is the break-up of a marriage. Just over one-forth of this sample responded that divorce or separation was a problem related to their drinking. This statistic does not tell whether the woman's drinking caused the divorce or separation, but it does directly relate problem drinking to marital dissolution and is consistent with the demographic picture presented in the previous section.

Studies have consistently found that marriage moderates levels of drinking for both men and women in the short term. However, there is a growing body of clinical evidence and survey findings, which demonstrate that long-term marriage protects male, but not female, heavy drinkers from the untrammeled practice of their addictive behavior and from the full consequences of such drinking (Hanna 1991; Power and Estaugh 1990). Whereas heavy-drinking men reduce their current drinking levels as a function of longer marriage, heavy-drinking women do not. Another study by Harford, Hanna, and Faden in 1994 examined the National Longitudinal Survey of Labor Market Experience in Youth and also found evidence to support the conclusion that men reduce their current levels of drinking as a function of longer marriage, but women's drinking increases. This same study provides three possible explanations for the increase in drinking among married women: 1) women become more isolated in marriage than men, 2) women drink more heavily over time as their responsibilities and roles decrease, and 3) women drink heavily to cope with unhappy marriages.

In addition to the reasons discussed above for a woman's increased drinking, another explanation may include the role of the other family members and their response to the alcoholic wife and mother. A respondent from this sample had the following experience and insight into the situation:

> While stationed in -------------- I met and married my husband who was the son of an alcoholic and in total denial of his father's alcoholism. Even though his father had died of alcoholic cirrhosis of the liver my husband until this day still denies that he was an alcoholic. My husband and I drank together and he became my greatest enabler even denying that I was an alcoholic when I came into AA. He was sure that I was going through "the change of life." He is an Italian and considers it shameful if your wife has a drinking problem. A "man" is supposed to control all the family problems. I have since learned that the woman who drinks at home alone is frequently protected by her family and prevented from getting help because of the belief that they are doing what is best for her.

Data from a longitudinal study conducted between 1981 and 1986 were analyzed by Wilsnack et al. (1994), and they concluded that for women who are problem drinkers, drinking is a risk factor for subsequent divorce or separation. However, these same women often reported a decrease in drinking after separation or divorce, suggesting that the heavy drinking and problem marriage were mutually reinforcing. Similarly, it is still unclear as to whether a woman's drinking is a cause, consequence, or accompaniment of divorce or separation. Another analysis of divorce rates from 1933 to 1984 concluded that divorce rates influence alcohol consumption but not the reverse (Magura and Shapiro 1988).

Other problems related to alcoholism include loss of a job; homelessness; and loss of their children. Given the high education and income levels of women in this sample, it is not expected that many women would lose their jobs, homes, or children. However, alcoholism is devastating, and the circumstances in which alcoholic women find themselves can be harsh regardless of their socio-economic status. The following is an excerpt from a respondent's story illustrating how her last days drinking were filled with abuse from her husband and ultimately the loss of her children. She recounts:

> And then I entered a living hell. Daily ranting and raving directed at me, sometimes lasting until 3:00 am—sometimes with a tape recorder shoved in my face to catch my responses to 50 questions. My shrink said exercise reduces stress so I walked. And walked and walked. My husband hired a private investigator to follow me. He had me take at-home Breathalyzer tests. I discovered a hidden camera on the arts and crafts shelves in the dining room. I was locked out of the upstairs and downstairs. I reached a level of despair that caused me to pray to a God I had abandoned when I moved out of my parents house. On my walks around the neighborhood, I prayed and prayed and I'd feel peace when I arrived back at the house. It was only momentary peace. We both knew it had to end but the house belonged to his parents and I didn't want to be accused of abandoning my children—he began to accompany us on our walks to school fearing I'd kidnap them. March 9th he locked me out. I moved in with my parents and the next day, I was served a restraining order—my husband went before a judge and claimed I hit him to ensure custody. A week later, in court, the judge dismissed my 2 ½ months of sobriety because he felt very few people successfully quit on their own; without a support group I was doomed to relapse and he awarded custody of my children to my husband. For the second time in my life, my heart was truly broken. I lost my identity. I was Sarah and Tommy's mom; that was what I wanted to be and loved being. I entered the rooms of AA a shell of a person, filled with nothing but anger and resentment.

Dual Addiction

Finally, dual addiction, being addicted to more than one drug, was common among women in this survey. Nearly half of these now well-educated, successful and economically prosperous women abused another drug in addition to alcohol.[4] The drugs they abused cover a fair portion of the gamut of legal and illegal substances (see table 2.2).

The most reported drug abused, in addition to alcohol, is cocaine. These women reflect the continued trend of cocaine abuse in America. Cocaine use and abuse in the U.S. skyrocketed in the 1980s, and it continues to be widely used in America today. Initially cocaine was perceived as a designer drug used among the affluent and as a "recreational" drug among the middle class. However, the abuse of and addiction to the drug became more apparent over time. In different forms, the drug was "pushed" in low-income, urban environments, creating devastating medical, emotional, and social problems. Many young minority women suffer the grave effects of cocaine addiction, including the phenomenon known as the "crack baby" (a baby born addicted to cocaine). The crack baby is to cocaine addition what fetal alcohol effect is to alcohol addiction, and both create life-long complications for the babies or victims of the condition. However, the babies are not the only victims; often the mothers carry this guilt for their entire lifetime. One respondent tells of her guilt, specifically related to the birth of her second child:

> And after the alcohol had really taken hold, there was a second girl, who was not quite as fortunate as her sister. She was born with Fetal Alcohol Effect. She later was diagnosed with attention deficit disorder at about four years of age and was put on medication, which helped. My daughter is slightly above normal in intelligence but had developmental anomalies in sequencing, in fine and gross motor control, and has dysgraphia. She is also manic depressive. After I was sane and sober, I began to advocate for special services for her but also found it harder to "hide" what had caused her condition. My daughter read the phrase "Fetal Alcohol Effect" from her file left open by a school guidance counselor. She has never been able to fully forgive me. She graduated from a licensed professional school several months ago, but I was not invited and I have not seen or heard from her since. The amount of guilt I harbored for the damage done to this child was so great and so long lasting that it became necessary for me to do another 4th step, just on that guilt, alone.

Next to cocaine use, barbiturates or prescription drugs were the most commonly reported drug used and abused by women in this survey. Often affiliated with the middle-class woman, minor tranquilizers or "sleeping pills" have been abused by housewives and women of similar circumstances for years. Similarly, stronger drugs such as Valium have become widely prescribed, and the physiological addiction has been overlooked until recently, because drugs of this type have typically been prescribed to women who have experienced anxiety and other nervous conditions. Therefore, women have been treated as if their symptoms were psychosomatic, and they were not considered credible when they reported signs of addiction. Moreover, addiction to such drugs leads to increased levels of isolation and other related problems. For many years, this form of addiction went undetected, because it was not an illegal drug. Moreover, the addiction created pain and suffering mostly for the individual user, and it did not seem to generate larger social problems.

In addition to cocaine and prescription narcotics, women in this sample also reported that marijuana was a drug of abuse. About 14 percent reported having been addicted to marijuana. Although there exists a great deal of controversy over whether marijuana is addictive in the biomedical sense, the women in this sample did not hesitate to identify it as a substance they were addicted to. One woman offered the response that she was also addicted to "marijuana, pot; I smoked it every day for eighteen years and it is addictive." Another woman qualified her response by stating that she had "smoked marijuana for ten years but had no problem stopping and used cocaine and did not have a problem stopping." Whatever their experience, marijuana was a popular drug that accompanied alcohol addiction among the women in this survey.

Conclusion

The women in this survey reveal certain similarities to the general demographic patterns that have already been established between women and alcoholism, but they also are very different in a number of important ways. These alcoholic women are similar to the general cross-section of American women who drink heavily in terms of race, age, marital status, and employment status. They are middle-aged white women, the majority of whom have either never been married or have been divorced or separated. On the other hand, as a group they are well educated, are employed in non-traditional occupations, enjoy high status positions, and earn high personal and household incomes. While it is not certain exactly what the causal relationship is between this demographic profile and alcoholic drinking, it is clear that in spite of their current well placed socio-economic position, all of these women have had to overcome many emotionally difficult experiences in their past in order to have sobriety today.

The problems women in general and this sample specifically experience as alcoholics are numerous and varied. Alcoholic women have high rates of past sexual abuse, they are often surrounded by alcoholism in their families, many problems go hand-in-hand with being an alcoholic woman, and many women are addicted to more than just alcohol. As a result of these conditions and circumstances, women alcoholics suffer from an accumulation of other difficulties and problems (depression, social embarrassment, loss of friends, suicidal thinking, poor health and so on) that not only make it difficult for women to get sober, but also make up part of the emotional "baggage" that women bring into AA with them. Women begin to address these emotional issues once in recovery and, in fact, as the next five chapters will illuminate, recovery becomes more than simply just not drinking but becomes a life-long process of self discovery and personal empowerment.

Notes

[1] The AA 2004 Membership Survey includes both men and women.

[2] To see a more detailed discussion of the relationship between parental substance abuse and influence on offspring within this sample, see Sanders, 2003.

[3] The National Institute of Mental Health funded an epidemiological study of the prevalence and incidence of psychiatric disorders in the U.S. It included a sample size of over 20,000 people. See Hezler, Burnham, & McEvoy (1991).

[4] Seventy-one women (44.1% of the AA sample) reported affirmatively that they had been addicted to another drug in addition to alcohol.

3
Women in Recovery

This chapter focuses on the extent to which this sample of women participates in AA and the larger twelve-step movement. Based on the active participation women in the past have had in AA, as was discussed in Chapter 1, I argue that women in AA continue to be active and engaged members of AA and the larger recovery community. Not only have women historically been active members of AA, but they have created their own space inside AA—women-only AA meetings. As has been discussed previously, women-only AA meetings were created by women as a response to the male-dominated culture in AA. Today, women-only meetings are widespread throughout AA, and, although they are very similar to mixed-gender AA meetings, clear differences can be found. Similarly, although AA membership is still made up of two men for every one woman, women make up the overwhelming majority of the membership in related twelve-step recovery groups such as Al-Anon, Co-Dependents Anonymous (CoDA), and Adult Children of Alcoholics (ACA).[1]

In addition to attending other twelve-step programs, women also seek professional treatment outside of AA. According to the Substance Abuse and Mental Health Administration (2000), women are three times more likely to seek substance abuse treatment than are men. Moreover, women are more likely to visit a mental health clinic or see a therapist or psychiatrist for help with an emotional problem than are their male counterparts. These data point to a strong likelihood that women are actively modifying the recovery environment to fit their gender-specific needs. Therefore, this research will measure the extent to which women's participation in AA is related to their sense of empowerment.

Several variables serve as indicators that measure women's involvement in AA and other forms of treatment. First, women's overall involvement in AA will be measured by women's length of sobriety in AA and frequency of attendance at mixed meetings of AA. Secondly, women's involvement in women-only meetings of AA will be measured by the frequency that women attend women-only AA meetings and will measure their preferences concerning attendance at women-only AA meetings. The reasons women attend women-only meetings will also be discussed. Thirdly, other means by which women help themselves both inside and outside of AA will be described. Specific measures include the activities women engage in to help their recovery in AA, treatment sought outside of AA, and alcoholic women's participation in other twelve-step programs. By use of these measures and by describing and discussing other activities and practices women use to make the recovery environment more agreeable and effective for them, it will be possible to arrive at a clear sense of how women empower themselves inside women's groups of AA.

Length of Time in Sobriety

Women in this survey were asked to report approximately how long they have been a member of AA since their last drink. Qualifying "since their last drink" measures uninterrupted sobriety time. This is an important measure, because many members of AA relapse (go back to drinking) one or more times before they achieve long-term sobriety. Out of this sample of 167 women, the average length of time in AA is eight years. AA's general membership also has an average of eight years sobriety. The AA literature and culture emphasizes the fact that "this is a one-day-at-a-time program." This helps the "newcomers" to recognize that, although sobriety is difficult to obtain, it can be done by not drinking one day at a time. It is often heard in AA meetings that beginners should go to meetings, pray if they can, and get a sponsor. These suggestions are believed to help a beginner to get a foothold on sobriety. Eventually, a solid length of time without a drink and membership in AA is thought to allow for a more stable and happy existence in sobriety, especially when compared with "newcomers" who have little by way of either sober time or serenity.

In this survey, just over 15 percent would be considered newcomers or have less than a year of sobriety in AA. This sample appears to have more mature members (those with time sober) compared to AA in general, as its membership survey reflects just over a quarter of its membership with less than a year of sobriety. However, both surveys look more alike as members report longer lengths of sobriety. In fact, both AA as a whole and this particular sample of women from AA have over one-third of its membership with ten or more years of sobriety. In comparison to those with little sobriety, those with long–term sobriety are sometimes referred to as "old timers." This group is made up of women who are often sought after to help the so-called newcomers to AA (see table 3.1).

**Table 3.1 Comparison of the length of time in AA between women in AA
& the AA Membership Survey (percent)**

Variable/Value	Women in AA	AA Membership
Length of Time in AA		
Less than one year	15.2	26
1 - 5 years	28.5	24
5 - 10 years	20.6	14
More than 10 years	35.7	36
Total N	(167)	(7,500)

*Source: AA's Membership Survey (2004). Note: AA's Membership
Survey data includes both women and men.*

Attendance at Mixed vs. Women-Only AA Meetings

The majority of women sampled in this survey attend AA meetings that
are open to both men and women. Not only do they attend mixed
meetings, but they do so with great frequency (one or more times a
week). Over three quarters attend mixed meetings at least once a week
and, of these, over 60 percent attend mixed meetings at least two times a
week. There is even a proportion, a quarter, of these women that attend a
mixed meeting between four to seven days a week, which is a lot by any
measure. In fact, AA's membership survey shows that average
attendance by its membership is two meetings per week. Particular to
this sample of women, only a minuscule percentage, less than 2.5
percent, never attend a mixed meeting.

While these women attend many mixed meetings, they also attend a
lot of women-only meetings of AA. The majority of women in this
study, 90 percent, attend women's AA meetings one or more times a
week. Of these, over one-half attend once per week, and one-third
frequent two to three meetings per week. There is no doubt that these
women are frequenting both mixed and women-only AA meetings. In
fact, almost four-fifths of these women attend both a mixed AA meeting
and a women-only AA meeting at least once per week. This rate of
attendance clearly demonstrates that these women are comfortable in
mixed as well as women-only meetings.

Table 3.2 Frequency of attendance at AA meetings by women in AA (percent)

Variable/Value	Women in AA
Attendance at Mixed AA Meetings	
Everyday or nearly everyday	9.6
4 – 5 times per week	14.4
2 – 3 times per week	40.0
Once a week	15.0
Less than once per week	18.6
Never	2.4
Attendance at Women-only AA meetings	
Everyday or nearly everyday	1.8
2 – 5 times per week	34.1
Once a week	54.5
Less than once per week	9.6
Never	0
Total N	(167)

Source: Women in AA sample.

However, it is remarkable that women attend women's meetings as often as they do, given the scarcity of women's meetings compared to mixed meetings. The ratio of women's meetings to mixed meetings listed in the "Where and When" directory for the Eastern Metropolitan Area lists fewer than sixty women-only meetings held weekly, as compared to approximately 2000 meetings held weekly, overall. Women-only meetings make up only 3 percent of the total pool of AA meetings. It appears, then, that women in AA actively seek out and support women-only meetings. This may be seen as evidence that women have in fact adapted AA culture to create an environment that meets their specific needs, founding women's meetings to supplement the mixed meetings with a unique recovery environment of their own.

Reasons for Attending Women-Only AA Meetings

The reasons that the women in this study gave for attending women's meetings support my argument that women in AA create and value their own unique recovery environment. In general, members of AA believe that a primary reason that they have been able to get sober is that they have worked with other alcoholics. The basic format of AA meetings involves alcoholics sharing "their experience, strength, and hope" with one another. In meetings, alcoholics relate what it was like to be an active alcoholic, what finally brought them to AA, and what it is like now, in recovery. By listening to other alcoholics "tell their stories," alcoholics, and especially newcomers to AA, are able to form a "deep identification" with the storyteller. Empathy develops as a result of the mutual experience of being an alcoholic (Denzin 1987). According to the responses they have provided, the women in this sample not only understand the need to identify with another alcoholic, but they also embrace the benefits that can be derived from developing a deep identification with the particular experiences of other alcoholic women. In fact, the women in this sample list their number one reason for attending women-only meetings is to learn from other women who have had similar experiences.

This need to form close connections with other women alcoholics in order to stay sober and also to enhance the quality of their sobriety is evident in the responses these women chose as to why they attend women's meetings. Almost 75 percent of the women selected responses that relate to building connections with other women. Only when more specific concerns, such as meeting a sponsor or wanting a meeting that was accepting of a woman's lesbian sexual orientation, came into play did the response rate on choices connected with establishing relations with other women drop off significantly.[2] All of the remaining responses reflect a very strong sense of identification with other women, a felt need to bond with other alcoholic women in sobriety, and a greater degree of comfort and reassurance in discussing personal matters with other women (see table 3.3). All of these reasons suggest that women in AA recognize a gender difference in both the content and styles of communication between themselves and the men in AA. If, as has been asserted, AA is a mutual aid society, then it makes sense for members of AA to seek help from people similar to themselves (Vourakis 1989). That is certainly the underlying idea behind the Twelfth Step, which was the foundational experience of Bill W. and Dr. Bob.[3] This is precisely what the women in this sample are expressing, when they give such high

Table 3.3 Summary of reasons to attend women-only AA meetings by women in AA (percent)

Variable/Value	Women in AA
Reasons to Attend Women-Only AA Meetings	
To learn from other women who have had similar experiences	85.6
To socialize with other women in the program	73.7
To seek encouragement and support from women in AA	73.7
To build closer relationships with women in recovery	72.5
To talk about issues that are of more interest to women than men	61.7
To discuss intimate issues of recovery in a safe environment	59.3
To help new female members of AA	57.5
To express emotion without embarrassment	50.9
To meet with my sponsor	22.8
Other	9.0
To discuss my sexual orientation as a lesbian	7.2
Total N	(167)

Note: Respondents not limited to one answer only.

response rates to reasons for attending women-only meetings, such as learning from, socializing with, gaining support from and giving support to other women alcoholics. All of these reasons, which showed up on nearly three quarters of the surveys, reflect a sense of identification and mutual understanding, and a desire to build even closer relationships with women in recovery.

Meeting Preference

It is clear that this sample of women value women-only AA meetings, but do they prefer women-only meetings to mixed meetings? Although they find many reasons to attend women-only meetings, these women do not necessarily favor those meetings over others. In fact, women in this sample are evenly divided in their preference for women's meetings as opposed to mixed meetings of AA.

Breaking down further their reasons for preferring women-only meetings reveals that a quarter of the women who reported a preference for women's meetings attribute this to the fact that they feel more comfortable in a women's meeting. Women reported feeling safer, closer to women, and feeling as though they can trust women in women-only meetings. The safety issue was mentioned by several women in their comments on women's meetings, often in conjunction with the fact that they feel closer bonds with other women in AA than they do with male alcoholics in recovery in AA. Characteristic statements along these lines include: "I feel closer to the women and safer in general," and "I feel more connected and in a safe environment to express myself." In a similar vein, one woman noted that "there's a bonding with other women," while another simply feels "more trusting of women." Often these women feel freer to discuss sensitive issues in front of other women. One notes that she feels "safer to discuss what is really going on with me." Another expresses anxiety over men's reactions, but with women she "can share embarrassing experiences without feeling the men would laugh at me." Yet another prefers women's meetings, when she is "more vulnerable," because she feels "safe discussing my issues." Not unexpectedly, one of the most sensitive issues and one that often leads these women alcoholics to prefer women's meetings has to do with sexuality. One woman feels that women's motives are less ambiguous, so she is "more comfortable with women than men—as men often have mixed intentions." For another woman the extreme sensitivity of one of her core issues led her to prefer women's meetings: "I am working on childhood sexual issues and do not feel safe in mixed meetings." Another put the matter right on the table, noting, "I just feel more comfortable discussing sex." Perhaps the crux of all these considerations is contained in another woman's beautifully phrased summation: "I get closer to my truth in the loving, safe environment" of a women's meeting.

Women also reported that they felt they could speak about women-related issues and that they preferred the style of communication in women's meetings. One woman writes that, "Women are less likely to just mouth AA platitudes and are more likely to talk about the application of AA principles to real life situations." Another woman notes a macho edge to men in AA: "Most men in AA seem concerned with proving that they were the worst drunk of all and are uncomfortable with discussing spiritual matters." Another woman takes the men at their word, writing that "Men sometimes speak about their problems communicating. This doesn't relate to me so I'd rather go to women's meetings to hear about things I can relate to in order to learn." Others focus on the positive elements of attraction to women's meetings. One writes that, "I feel women understand the feelings and problems I deal with on an everyday basis." Another feels "more at ease discussing 'any topic' in a women's meeting." A third woman attends women's meetings "primarily to discuss women related issues." Another woman concludes simply that she has "a freedom to discuss personal matters other women would understand."

The final reason that women gave for preferring women-only meetings is that women are more honest than men. They find franker, more open discourse and less posing. A representative sampling of their opinions includes the statements that "women are more honest—I relate to them better," and that there is "more honest sharing by me and others" and "a higher level of honesty in women's meetings." One woman finds "it easier to express my concerns in women's meetings." Another "can't get to many meetings, so the one I do go to each week is a women's meeting because it is always a very honest and open meeting." Many find that men get in the way of what they come to AA for. Women's meetings are better, they think, because there is "less positioning, more empathy, and greater similarity of experience in a women's meeting" and because "women do not have to first establish their status." Put simply, "no male distractions." One woman summed it up in very positive terms: "I get so much direct experience, strength, and hope from the women about the issues in my life."

Although already demonstrated in their reasons for attending women-only meetings, some of the women specifically state that they prefer women-only meetings, because they have a desire to connect with other women alcoholics. Again, the women in this sample recognize and seek a deep identification with other women in AA based on two identities. The first identity is that of an alcoholic in recovery as Denzin (1987) has described, and the second identity is that of a woman in recovery. A woman opening a women-only AA meeting illustrated the intersection of these two identities, when she said "I already know you know what it is like to be an alcoholic and you already know what it is like to be a woman, therefore I can share with you all at a level of understanding that I can nowhere else." This statement reflects the consciousness shared by many women in AA. An excerpt from one of the respondents to this survey speaks to the evolution of her connection with women. She writes:

> As a woman, I have found great comfort in connecting with other women in recovery. In my drinking and using days, I found women to be threatening and believed they could not give me anything I thought I needed. Today, because of women in AA, I know that I can express my feelings in a more honest way than I can in a mixed meeting. For

example, I just had a hysterectomy and was able to share in women's meetings about the loss of not ever having children. I got so much support for which I am grateful. My surgery may not have had anything to do with alcoholism, but the tools of the program have many applications for life-changing experiences.

This same respondent adds, "Connecting with women in the program has also helped me to learn to trust myself and others again. If I cannot trust others, it is more difficult for me to trust God. Without a trust in God and a belief that I deserve his love, I am doomed."

Other women express similarly profound experiences. One woman attributes her sobriety to developing connections with women in AA. She shares:

I started to develop friendships in the groups, especially with women. The women's meetings really "spoke" to me. I was asked to join a group of recovering women meeting once a week for dinner and friendly conversation. I have been attending this group regularly for 9 years and think this has been one of the reasons for my now 11 ½ years of sobriety.

Another woman comments:

Clearly, for me, women's meetings are the most significant because of the issues that women raise. I have heard other women say, and I agree, that somehow one's drinking does not seem the same as or legitimate when looked at in terms of men's stories. Women do not put the same weight on the same events or issues. I believe there are women's issues and men's issues.

A third woman explains how she finally came to a women's AA meeting after being involved with a man in AA and living through a violent assault. She writes:

I met a man at an AA picnic. He was sober only a few months, but he had been sober for seven years previously, so I deemed him GOD, and we started dating. I got drunk after seven months, for one day, but quickly sobered up so I wouldn't lose that man. I also lived through an attack at my home. A man with a huge knife and a ski mask threatened to kill me if I didn't do what he wanted. Thanks to my 'undying love' for the man I was dating, and thanks to my own still self-destructive behavior, I told the attacker that he should just go ahead and kill me. I got away. The next night I went to a women's AA meeting and discovered the reason for AA: nearly every woman in that room had been raped, too. I felt scared, but I knew I could live through it, as they had.

Women who prefer mixed meetings also provided more extensive written comments on their experiences as alcoholic women in recovery through AA. Even those women in this sample who do not prefer women's meetings recognize gender differences. These women, however, are either neutral or enthusiastic about the male perspective. Some value women-only meetings, but benefit from mixed meetings, as well. One woman writes that:

> Women-only meetings will always have a place in my program but are not necessarily preferred. I feel the need to have both kinds of meetings as part of my program and benefit from both. I like a good message of recovery whether it's in a mixed or a women's group. I get the help I need from every AA meeting, not only women's meetings.

Other women actively prefer gender diversity. One remarks that:

> I get enormous insight from both types of meetings. Each type has valuable and unique aspects each of which is necessary for a full range of views of recovery. I am happy to attend both and need the mix of both.

Other respondents remark that they can learn about men by attending mixed meetings. One woman notes that she needs, "to learn to interact with both sexes; I think it is important to socialize with men as well as women; I need to know men can have the same feelings about their 'ism' and hearing men helps to demystify them—helps me learn about men in a safe environment." This comment echoes those by women who prefer women-only meetings, because they feel safer, freer, and more intimate and honest. The key aspect of meeting preference is a sense of comfort and security, because that environment is essential to the honesty required by the recovery project. Some women find that sense of ease and comfort in mixed meetings; others in women's meetings. Either way, these women are shaping the environments necessary to regain control of their lives.

Among the women surveyed for this study, there is a small group of only three women who react negatively to women's meetings. Two of the women remarked about women being "whiny." One woman writes, "I don't have the patience for much whining," and another woman states, "I feel comfortable in both meetings but some women-only meetings tend to be very whiny. There are lots of sob stories and not enough of *working in a solution*" (italics in the original). The third woman dislikes what she perceives to be an excessive amount of time spent talking about the problems the women have with men. As she put it, "I do always have at least one women's meeting in my schedule; however women can get too much into men issues." Paradoxically, these complaints confirm that women have created their own cultural environment within the larger AA culture. For some women, however, that special culture is not something that they can relate to.

Finally, a couple of women remarked that they had no preference for women's meetings, but that their feelings about women's meetings fluctuate, depending on how they feel at a particular time or what they want from an AA meeting. For example, one woman reflects, "I prefer mixed meetings for Big Book and Step meetings to get everyone's experience. But I need women's meetings for emotional support and honest interpersonal relationships." For two other women, it is more a function of where they are emotionally. As one of them put it, "It really depends on how I'm feeling at that time, and it depends what is going on in my life." Another woman explains in more depth, "When I first got sober I found it great and even necessary to go to mixed meetings to hear men share from the heart. Now, it doesn't make much difference to me. I go to some mixed and some women's meetings. I pick them more due to quality of sobriety than what sex [is present]." This flexibility in meeting choice confirms Vourakis' findings in her 1989 study that women attend meetings where other women are in the same stage of recovery as themselves (Vourakis 1989). Overall, even those women who do not prefer women's meetings to mixed meetings still recognize and value the difference between the two.

Help Yourself in Recovery

It is a truism within AA that alcohol is but a symptom of the problems that alcoholics have living "life on life's terms." As it has been phrased, "Drinking didn't make me who I was; who I was made me drink." Hence, a very important part of an individual's recovery involves identifying and addressing the whole range of psychological, social, and spiritual aspects of her life that need attention, so that she can live, as AA literature has it, "happy, joyous and free." The alcoholic women in this sample engage in a wide range of activities that focus on the problems they bring with them into AA. As has been discussed in an earlier chapter, many of these women have experienced severe abuse in their lives. Oftentimes, alcoholics drink to repress memories of this abuse or to anesthetize themselves. Part of the recovery process, especially in early sobriety, involves letting the memories and emotional reactions to this abuse come to the surface, so that they can be addressed. As it is put in the rooms of AA, "you're only as sick as your secrets." In AA terms, much of this is dealt with in the Fourth and Fifth Steps. Many alcoholics, however, feel the need to address these issues further. In this sample, fully 90 percent of these women have found it worthwhile to identify and clarify emotional wounds that must be healed for them to experience the full benefits of getting sober.

After identifying emotional areas that need healing, the second most frequent area addressed by women in this sample is the need to develop healthy personal relationships. Given the problems these women have already faced, it is not surprising that a substantial portion of the women in this sample, 87 percent, have devoted time and attention to developing their relationships with others. The women's stories, told in later chapters, clearly illustrate how much work these women put into creating better relationships once in recovery.

Even women without the scarring traumas of abuse find it useful and beneficial to augment their recovery by working on other areas of their lives. For example, more than four out of five of the women surveyed have sought to improve themselves and the quality of their lives by eliminating self-destructive behaviors and have worked toward improving their physical health. A smaller, but still significant, proportion of these women are also trying to enhance their sobriety by working on recovery from other addictions, by developing their job skills, and by improving their parenting skills.[4] Additionally, a small group of these women are finding it worthwhile to expand their knowledge of their ancestry and familial heritages by learning more about their ethnic identity (see table 3.4). Recovery from alcoholism encompasses many aspects of a woman's life and clearly is not limited merely to not drinking. These women address the problems in their lives and this helps them to overcome more than just not drinking. These women are indeed, building on their experiences in AA to construct a broader program of recovery of self.

Finally, it should be noted briefly that almost three-quarters of the women surveyed are working at extending their "conscious contact with a power greater than themselves," by developing their spiritual lives beyond what they have done in this regard in AA. Although the Twelve Steps introduce the spiritual aspects of recovery, each woman designs and builds her own personal relationship with a higher power in the way in which she is comfortable. More discussion about spirituality will follow in the upcoming chapters.

**Table 3.4 Summary of helpful activities engaged in by women in AA
(percent)**

Variable/Value	Women in AA
What Helps Their Recovery	
Identify emotional areas that need healing	89.8
Develop healthy relationships	87.4
Attempt to reduce self-destructive behaviors	84.4
Seek better physical health	80.2
Develop a spiritual life beyond AA	74.3
Work on recovery from other addictions	52.7
Develop better parenting skills	36.5
Develop occupational skills	31.7
Learn about my ethnic identity	5.4
Other	7.2
Total N	(167)

Note: Respondents not limited to one answer only.

Only twelve women marked "other" in response to what they do to help their recovery and the list of activities was varied. For example, one woman reports that she does volunteer work, takes exercise classes, and generally keeps busy. A second respondent shares that she seeks nutritional counseling and behavioral change. Similarly, a third woman notes that she stays away from chemicals in her diet like MSG, hydrogenated fat and eats only healthy whole foods, because she experiences severe depression and aggression when she eats MSG. This same respondent adds "taking vitamins improves my brain functioning and taking essential fatty acids like omega 3, 6, & 9's help [sic] me to think better and to feel better." Another woman mentions meditation, while another two women speak of sponsoring women in the program and practicing AA principles in all their affairs—all of which are related to spiritual development. All of these women seek to enhance their personal well being, and they do so through diverse means to target either emotional, interpersonal, or spiritual needs.

Outside Treatment

According to the National Institute on Drug Abuse (1991), women represent one-quarter of alcoholism clients in traditional treatment centers in the United States. This figure is comparable to other more recent statistics that continue to show that there are three times more male alcoholics than there are women. Hence, alcoholic women are proportionally represented in a very important vehicle for recovery, treatment centers. Moreover, alcoholic women also pursue avenues toward recovery other than traditional alcoholism programs, such as psychiatric services or personal physicians, when seeking treatment (Beckman and Kocel 1982). Similarly, women make up the majority of members in attendance at other twelve-step programs such as Al-Anon and Adult Children of Alcoholics (Mäkelä et al.1996; Rapping 1996).

Given the prevalence of past abuse, family histories of alcoholism, and the many other problems associated with alcoholism, it is expected that women in this sample would have sought professional treatment outside of AA. In fact, almost three-quarters of the women in this sample have sought outside help (see table 3.5). Far and away the most common form of professional treatment outside of AA involved seeing a therapist or psychiatrist. Well over half of these women, 62 percent, have seen a therapist or psychiatrist in addition to membership in AA. Typically, this type of practitioner will address many life issues in addition to alcoholism. These practitioners are often trained from a mental health perspective, and their training may or may not include awareness or focus on addictions.

No other form of professional treatment approaches the level of those who have sought counseling help of psychiatrists and therapists. Nonetheless, a substantial percentage, over a fifth of the women surveyed here had gone through outpatient rehabilitation. Patients in this structured form of substance abuse counseling often focus on specific aspects of recovery and the Twelve Steps. For example, one woman who had difficulty staying sober explained "I was referred to a relapse prevention therapy group, where we spent the next two years, once a week, doing something like a Fourth and Fifth Step on areas we assessed were *triggers* that would lead to relapse. The triggers were really *character defects*." (italics in the original) The "character defects" referred to here are part of the Fourth, Fifth, Sixth and Seventh Steps of AA, the phrase itself comes from the Sixth Step. Another 20 percent of these women had recourse to an inpatient or hospital program. This type of intervention is intensive and often combines a medical and a rehabilitation approach toward the treatment of addictions. One respondent describes the second inpatient program she went to before she finally stopped drinking. She exclaims, "This time I researched rehabs, having the luxury of being able to pay for any rehab, and picked ---- primarily because they used a holistic approach toward recovery. I spent twenty-eight days there and finally understood what recovery was about and what I needed to do." Another thirteen women reported having been in a residential program, which gives the woman a structured and safe environment in which to live while she begins her recovery. These programs vary in terms of length of stay and criteria for admission. Typically, however, a patient may live in a recovery home anywhere from three months to a year. Some programs focus on addiction recovery specific to women and expand on their services by allowing small children to live with their mother, while she is in treatment. In addition, nine women reported attending an educational or drunk-driving program. Alcoholics typically only go to these types of programs, if they have been arrested for a drunk-driving offense. Some individuals attend before they go to court in hopes that they can get a reduced sentence. Others attend only after being court ordered to do so. Finally, five women marked "other" under treatment attended outside of AA. Two of these women reported attending the Caron Foundation for Co-Dependency which is a specialized intensive residential program that focuses on developing healthy relationships with one's self and others.

Although just over three-quarters of the women in AA sampled for this research have sought outside treatment, it is not known whether the women in this sample sought treatment outside of AA before entry into AA or in addition to membership in AA. Often, members of AA are referred to AA from a professional treatment provider or facility. AA's own membership survey reports that 58 percent of its members were referred to AA by a treatment facility, counseling agency, or other health care professional and that 64 percent of AA members have received some type of treatment or counseling including medical, psychological, or spiritual, before coming to AA (Alcoholics Anonymous 2004). It is clear that outside help is not uncommon among alcoholics in AA and that this particular sample of women is not unlike AA's own account of membership activity in regards to outside treatment.

Other Twelve-Step Programs

Just as alcoholics often find it necessary to take other steps toward self-improvement and also to seek out professional help, so they often discover that other twelve-step programs will help them deal effectively with their problems. Out of the 167 women in this study, sixty-seven or

40 percent have attended other twelve-step programs (see table 3.5). The most frequented twelve-step program outside of AA, attended by two-thirds of these women, is Al-Anon. Founded in 1951 by Bill Wilson's wife, Lois, based on the Twelve Steps and structured much like AA, Al-Anon was the first twelve-step program outside of AA. Since alcoholism is a family disease that affects everyone living with the alcoholic, spouses of alcoholics are often profoundly affected by their spouse's alcoholism. Often they try to control or manage the behavior of the alcoholic and the problems that arise because of alcoholic behavior. This can involve hiding or pouring out bottles of liquor, lying to bosses about the reason the alcoholic is missing work, trying to nag the alcoholic into different behavior and so on. Today this is known as "enabling" the alcoholic. Al-Anon originated as a program for these spouses of alcoholics. It uses the principles of AA's Twelve Steps to focus the wives on spirituality as a means of handling their problems with alcohol, which take the form of their husband's alcoholism.[5] In short, members of Al-Anon develop their own spiritual program independent of their spouses and focus on their own personal development. For many in Al-Anon, and especially for many women, this is the first time they have looked at themselves and begun to take control of their own lives rather than focusing on controlling the alcoholic. Spouses learn to detach from the alcoholic and learn to not enable or cover for the alcoholic, at the same time they learn to stop "nagging" the alcoholic. In sum, Al-Anon teaches the spouse of an alcoholic that only the alcoholic can help himself and that it is not the spouse's fault that her husband is an alcoholic, nor is it her job to get the husband sober.

In terms of the forty-five women in this sample who also attend Al-Anon, they suffer both from their own alcoholism and from that of their husbands or mates. Some women came to AA from Al-Anon. They had begun attending Al-Anon due to their husband's drinking and only then realized that they too were alcoholic. One woman admits, "I went to Alanon [sic], sure that my husband was much worse than me." Another woman expresses that "It took me 10 years in Al-Anon to realize that I had never admitted I was powerless over alcohol." This sequencing of twelve-step recovery is common, and AA members call it "coming in through the back door." For other women in recovery, they may have a family member who still drinks alcoholically. Once they have begun to get control of their drinking and their lives, they see more clearly their inability to control the drinking of others. It is at this point that they seek out Al-Anon meetings as a way to deal with their powerlessness. Whether they come to AA from Al-Anon or the other way around, many women in this sample find both programs necessary to deal with the problem of alcohol in their lives, and it is easier to integrate the two recovery programs into their lives, because the programs are based on the same principles.

Of the subgroups who attend more than one fellowship, exactly a quarter, also attended Narcotics Anonymous (NA). NA was the first twelve-step fellowship outside of AA to address substances other than alcohol and was founded in 1953 (Narcotics Anonymous 1983). Members of AA who were also addicted to other drugs started this alternative twelve-step program for the dual-addicted, since membership in AA required only a desire to stop drinking and did not include the desire to stop using other drugs.

Given the increase in drug use in the United States in the last half century, it is not surprising that the incidence of dual addiction for women has increased. In fact, polydrug abuse is now more common than abuse of alcohol alone or of a single drug (SAMHSA 1998). As a result, it is not surprising to find NA members in this sample, as well. As of 1992, NA was the largest twelve-step fellowship outside of AA and Al-Anon (Mäkelä et al. 1996).

The third most attended program for women in this sample is Adult Children of Alcoholics (ACA). This program is another twelve-step fellowship that helps individuals deal with the distorting and damaging effect of having an alcoholic in the family, in this case a parent. ACA teaches members that, as children of an alcoholic, they are not to blame for their parent's alcoholism, they should not try to "cure" the alcoholic, and they need to "work through" the emotional "baggage" they bring with them into adulthood that comes from having grown up in an unpredictable and sometimes violent environment. Although this resembles psychological counseling and therapy, it is not. As with the other twelve-step programs, ACA emphasizes a spiritual solution to these problems. Given that over 57 percent of the women in this sample were raised by an alcoholic parent, it is surprising that only twelve women out of 167 or 7 percent have attended ACA. This reflects minimal involvement, and not over-involvement, in the larger twelve-step movement. Only a handful of women reported attendance at twelve-step programs other than the three discussed in the preceding paragraphs. Eight women reported attending Overeaters Anonymous (OA), five women have attended Co-Dependents Anonymous (CoDA); and one woman reported that she has attended Chemical Dependency Anonymous (CDA). In addition, eight women reported that they attended other twelve-step fellowships not listed on the survey instrument. Six women have attended Debtors Anonymous in addition

Table 3.5 Seeking help outside of AA by women in AA (percent)

Variable/Value	Women in AA
Treatment Outside of AA	
Therapist/psychologist/psychiatrist	62.2
Outpatient rehabilitation	22.5
Inpatient/hospitalization	21.3
Residential	8.0
Education/Drunk Driver Program	5.0
Other	3.0
Total N	(164)
Attendance to Other Twelve Step Programs	
Al-Anon	27.0
Narcotics Anonymous	10.0
Adult Children of Alcoholics	7.0
Chemical Dependency Anonymous	6.0
Overeaters Anonymous	5.0
Other: Debtor's Anonymous	4.8
Co-dependency Anonymous	3.0
Total N	(165)

Note: Respondents not limited to one answer only.

to AA. One of the six noted that she has attended both Al-Anon and Debtor's Anonymous. Another woman has attended Sex and Love Addicts Anonymous. Finally, one woman has been an active member in another group addressing alcoholism that is not a twelve-step fellowship. This woman attended Women for Sobriety between the years 1981 to 1996.[6] Nineteen women out of 165, or just over 11 percent, have attended two or more twelve-step programs in addition to AA.

Overall, these findings suggest that women are neither passive when it comes to recovery nor uncritical when it comes to seeking outside help. Women in this sample utilize various means of support as they get sober. Over 70 percent of the women in this sample have sought professional treatment outside of AA, and just over 40 percent have attended other twelve-step programs in addition to AA. Moreover, the women in this sample are active in developing their personal well-being beyond just abstinence from alcohol and other substances. These women realize that recovery is more than admitting powerlessness over alcohol. They seek emotional, spiritual, and physical health and do so with varied resources and extra support when necessary.

Even after one has been sober for a while, other emotional supports may be needed. Without apology, one woman asserts:

> I sought professional counseling twice since my mother died. I had depression and grief issues and I needed to air things with a dispassionate, trained person. There are those who think that AA answers all questions, problems. I think there is a time and place for other help. Some people require medication for physical, mental and emotional problems. I believe that people should have the benefit of every kind of help that is available. So I am no 'hardliner' when it comes to seeking help outside of AA.

Another woman shares:

> I have had two 6-month sessions of therapy since coming back into the program and am on medication for depression. Both the therapy with two different but excellent women social workers familiar with the program and the drug therapy have been quite successful. Today I am confident and taking back responsibility for my life.

Yet another woman, who used a different form of help she found she needed while struggling to get and keep sobriety, relates that:

> After a month of trying everything suggested, the big book, meetings, calling, keeping a chip, the compulsions were just too strong and I put myself on Antabuse. This allowed me to play the game that while I was on it there was no point in drinking. When a compulsion came, I told myself that you can stop taking the medication and in a week you can drink. However, every night the compulsion would be gone and I would pop another pill and get one more day. I did this for a year, and finally the compulsion left me.

Lastly, one woman writes about her experience attending another mutual help group that was created specifically for female alcoholics. She states:

> My experience with Women For Sobriety has been very helpful and interesting. I went to several conferences in Quakertown and spent long weekends at these conferences exclusively in the company of other women in recovery. In my own group, we spent about two years talking about our mothers. This was not planned but we had a lot of issues with our mothers.

Each of these women unhesitatingly crafted a complete program that helped them deal with both alcoholism and life.

These findings do not substantiate the criticism put forth by Rapping (1996) that women become overly absorbed in the twelve-step culture. Although 40 percent of this AA sample has attended other twelve-step programs, only a handful of these women, five, have attended three or more twelve-step programs. This finding indicates that women seek out only those programs which they believe will really help them, and they do not simply consume the twelve-step culture by attending twelve-step fellowships that are not meaningful to them. Given the high figures for women in this sample who had alcoholic parents and who were addicted to another drug in addition to alcohol, the women in this sample seem to be under represented in other twelve-step programs and are not indiscriminately attending twelve-step programs.

The twelve-step programs which receive the most criticism from Rapping and others are those which deal with relationships. Very few women in this sample have attended Co-Dependents Anonymous (CoDA) or Sex and Love Addictions programs. These women have found or devised ways to address issues involving relationships, without having to have recourse to those two specialized twelve-step programs that have no specific connection with alcohol abuse or alcoholics. Their responses to the survey and the written replies provided by some of these women demonstrate that they have resolved problems connected with relationships by attending Al-Anon and ACA meetings and by discussing these issues within the context of AA, especially in women-only meetings. Therefore, it would seem that women who attend women's meetings of AA, Al-Anon and ACA are getting the recovery they need without having to branch out into other twelve-step programs. Women in this sample are also seeking out and finding help from other sources outside of the twelve-step programs, when they deem it necessary. If the crux of the criticisms leveled by Rapping and others is that women in twelve-step programs are encouraged to focus on themselves and to think of themselves as either being to blame for or the victim of some situation, then the experiences of the women surveyed for this study do not support those criticisms. These women have learned to focus on themselves as the only part of the problem they have any power to control, and they can then stop thinking of themselves as either the cause of or the solution for problems and circumstances beyond their control. These women have assimilated themselves to AA culture and AA culture to themselves.

Conclusion

In summary, the women in this sample are very active participants in the recovery process. They tend to have about eight years of sobriety on the average, and they attend both mixed meetings of AA and women-only meetings at least one or more times per week. The women in this sample attend women-only meetings, so that they can build connections with other women. For those women who specifically prefer women-only meetings, about half do so because they feel more comfortable, safer, and closer to women at these meetings. In addition to attending women-only meetings, the women in this sample help their recovery by identifying emotional areas that need healing, and they also want to develop healthy personal relationships. Women also report seeking help outside of AA, and this typically means a visit to a therapist or psychiatrist. Lastly, about 40 percent of this sample of women has attended other twelve-step programs, the most popular being Al-Anon. Taken together, all of these descriptive facts portray a group of women who bond with each other and in doing so have created their own supportive environment inside AA.

Notes

[1] All of these spin-off programs utilize the twelve-step principles and traditions, and they have similar organizational structures to that of AA.

[2] It could be argued that those other concerns–sponsorship by another woman and meetings accepting of lesbianism–are themselves reflections of a need to build closer relations with other women, too.

[3] Bill W. and Dr. Bob are the co-founders of Alcoholics Anonymous. Together, they found that by talking to each other, telling their story, and working together, they could stay sober. This experience of sharing their like dilemma with alcohol addiction becomes what is known today as Alcoholics Anonymous. See Alcoholics Anonymous (1976) for more information.

[4] In precise terms, 66 percent of those women who are mothers (92 out of 167) report helping their recovery by working at being better mothers.

[5] Typically, even today, the husband is the alcoholic, and the wife is the spouse attending Al-Anon.

---

[6] As was discussed earlier, Women for Sobriety is an alternative program to AA for women seeking recovery from alcoholism. It was initiated by a recovering alcoholic, Jean Kirkpatrick, who believed that alcoholic women suffered from low self-esteem and therefore needed a unique program outside of AA to address this, specifically.

4

Women's Struggle with Surrender: Steps One through Three

This chapter will discuss the specific experiences women have had with the first three steps (other steps will be discussed in succeeding chapters). The discussion here will restate the feminist critique of the Twelve Steps, will introduce the steps as they are generally understood within AA, and will then focus on these women's particular experiences with the first three steps. In order to provide a quantitative measure, the women were asked to rate on a four-point Likert scale how difficult it was to work a particular step. The same language was not used on every question, and not all of the Twelve Steps were included in the questionnaire. Rather, this research focuses on the steps that have been identified by feminists as potentially oppressive to women, the steps that are thought to accommodate gender sensitivity, and the steps that encourage a spiritual development and ongoing involvement in AA.

Steps One through Three are included, because they require the woman to give up power and to become dependent on something outside of herself. This process sounds anti-feminist. It is only in the last thirty years that women have begun to experience social equity and political power, and the gains they have registered have not been achieved by admitting powerlessness or by surrendering. Steps Four and Eight are included, because women have begun to modify these steps and work them from a gendered perspective. Finally, the way that women develop a spiritual program that fits their gender-specific needs is explored by means of questions about Step Eleven, and women's involvement in AA is gauged via questions about their experiences with the Twelfth Step. Taken together, it becomes possible to assess whether these women have experienced empowerment or an alternative form of disenfranchisement and powerlessness in place of their alcoholism.

Turning now to this sample of women in AA, almost 60 percent have "worked" the Twelve Steps. For most members of AA the steps are never completed in total. It is common, though, to refer to someone who has completed the first nine steps and is working the last three on a regular basis as a person who has "worked the steps." And, in fact, many women in this survey commented that the Twelve Steps are never complete, that they continually work them, and that it is an ongoing process. Depending on the step, some are used on a more frequent basis than others, and some are applied to certain areas of one's life more than others. Nonetheless, both AA literature and the comments of participants in this survey echo the idea that the Twelve Steps are principles and exercises that can be used on a daily basis.

The First Step

The First Step of AA reads, "We admitted we were powerless over alcohol—that our lives had become unmanageable." It is often said in AA meetings that "the only step you have to work perfectly is the First Step." By that, it is meant that, if the alcoholic does not give up alcohol absolutely, she is likely to drink again, and her life will become unmanageable again. Once an alcoholic has accepted her alcoholism and has admitted to her "innermost self" that she is unable to control her drinking, that she lacks the power to do so, she is ready to begin to do something about it. That is what the First Step is all about.

It is hardly surprising to find that these women in AA have had trouble admitting their powerlessness over alcohol. Almost 70 percent of the women who have completed this step had a hard time admitting to their problem. Almost one-third report their experience with this step as very difficult. By way of contrast, less than one-third of those women who have completed the First Step did not experience any difficulty at all (see table 4.1). However, those women who did not find the step problematic had already gone through a lot before they came to admit their alcoholism. Clearly, the First Step is one of the greatest hurdles for an alcoholic to surmount.

Those who found the First Step difficult write that they could not accept that they were powerless over alcohol. This was either due to their denial that they had a problem in the first place or because, after having admitted that they had a problem and after having begun to try to address it, they experienced chronic relapses. Some said that they thought they could "cure" themselves or control their drinking themselves. For many, it took several years and many hospitalizations to finally stop drinking.

The most remarkable statements came from those women who took a long time to finally stop drinking. The chronic nature of alcoholism, and the time and intensive efforts that it took for some women to complete the First Step are reflected clearly in their comments. One woman writes that she "was in 2 rehabs, immediately in a row, a 30 day program and then 3 months in a rehab for people of my profession. This allowed me more time to accept step 1." And even before the grueling bout with the initial stage of recovery, her "therapist had tried for months to get me to go to AA." Another woman wrote, "The 1st step took me 5 years to get it. I was in and out of rehab for 5 years until I finally stopped using." Still another woman responded, "I relapsed several times over several years before accepting complete powerlessness." Three other participants reported that it took them three and a half years, eight years, and ten years, respectively, before they finally stopped drinking. Another woman admitted, "It took me ten years in Al-Anon to realize that I had never admitted I was powerless over alcohol." Whatever the path, women who report having a difficult time with the First Step have fought the idea that they cannot drink, even after being exposed to AA or alcoholism treatment.

The clinical or professional literature which incorporates medical methodology with AA philosophy has a term for the resistance that alcoholics mount to acknowledging their addiction and the unmanageability in their lives. It is "denial." In treatment environments, the alcoholic is confronted with evidence of the chaos and unmanageability of her life and is challenged to think about the negative effects of alcohol and the impact alcohol has had on her life. Once the denial of the disease of alcoholism has been penetrated, the alcoholic can begin to look at her inability to drink normally and can begin to accept her powerlessness over alcohol.

The other main barrier to admitting their alcoholism and working the First Step that these women reported was a pattern of chronic return to their destructive habits. Among treatment professionals in the field of addictions, the term applied to this type of behavior is "relapse." By definition, relapse is drinking again after a period of abstinence. Most people do not refer to relapse, unless they have received treatment for alcoholism or have been exposed to AA. The more common language heard in AA is that a member has had a "slip." If an AA member goes out and drinks again, she has had a slip. In the earlier days of AA and even today, an old timer might say that another member of AA did not "slip," but chose to go out and "pick up," or drink again, implying that the individual is conscious of her actions and that drinking again is not an accident. Members of AA suggest to the newcomer that she stay away from slippery people, places, and things. By this they mean that the new AA member should stay away from people who are still drinking heavily, from places such as bars and liquor stores, and from things that are often associated with drinking. This advice is given to help protect the individual from placing herself in a situation that invites drinking or makes it difficult for the woman to resist drinking. Over time in the program of AA, an individual member can use her own discretion about such things and every woman's circumstances are different. Today, the treatment community applies these same suggestions to the treatment of alcoholism by educating the woman about how to identify people, places, and things that either triggered her drinking in the past or might cause her to drink again in the future. An example of the willingness to let go of people, places, and things is reflected in the following narrative provided by one of the participants in this survey:

> I threw myself into AA, got a sponsor, and attended meetings daily— sometimes twice a day. I was surrounded by recovering alcoholics who gave me their phone numbers, told me what to do, and helped me cope in my life without alcohol or drugs. I stopped socializing with my drinking friends, got rid of the booze and pot in my house, stayed out of bars, and bonded with another newcomer who just celebrated four years of sobriety.

This is the kind of transformed life style that both AA and the treatment community recommend for people trying to change their past behavior patterns.

Related to identifying slippery places, AA members tell newcomers to think through a drink before they pick up again. By this they mean for the individual to think past the romantic image or good feeling associated with drinking to what inevitably happens when the individual begins to drink. The AA member reminds the newcomer that the first drink will get them drunk—that for the alcoholic drinker the first drink will break down the resistance that the individual has been building up. And since one drink is never enough for an alcoholic, many more drinks will follow, and the alcoholic cycle will begin again. The newcomer is reminded that the nature of the disease of alcoholism will not allow her to have control over drinking, and it is only a matter of time before she will be drinking alcoholically again. Therefore, the alcoholic must think through the consequences of her drinking and continue to look at how her life has become unmanageable due to drinking. This cognitive approach to preventing relapse is found both in AA and in the context of professional treatment for alcoholism.

Another aspect of relapse prevention is to get a sponsor and make contacts with other people in AA. Again, the established AA member suggests to new members to get telephone numbers and to call another AA member before they pick up a drink. The idea is that, if a woman will just stop for a moment and make an AA contact, she will be reminded not to give into the compulsion of her disease and probably will be instructed to go to an AA meeting. Similarly, members of AA recommend strongly that newcomers find a sponsor, even a temporary sponsor, so that they have someone they can talk to directly about wanting to drink. In addition to immediate relapse intervention, making AA contacts and having a sponsor helps to bring a new member into the fellowship of AA. When a newcomer begins to develop friendships in AA and begins to use the fellowship of AA, this too helps to keep her strong and away from drinking again. Similarly, if a woman is involved in professional treatment, here too she will be encouraged to build a "network" of support, which includes using the fellowship of AA to help reduce her chances of relapse.

Among those women who found the First Step not difficult at all, most had already felt they were powerless over alcohol or that their lives were unmanageable. Their statements reflect this. One woman wrote, "I knew I was powerless—just didn't know what to do about it." Another "felt powerless over life." A third stated, "I knew I was an alcoholic and completely powerless." Yet another admitted, "My life was very much unmanageable." As another summed it up, "I knew I wasn't succeeding on my own." Other women were simply ready to give up the fight against alcohol and easily accepted the First Step once they came into AA. One wrote that "By the time I came to the 1st step, I was ready," while another "was ready to get the help I needed." Two women made virtually identical statements. One wrote that "By the time I got here I knew," compared with another's "By the time I got to AA it was obvious to me." Still other women referred to "hitting bottom" and therefore being accepting of the First Step. "Hitting bottom" is an often-used phrase in AA, which means that the individual has fallen so far as a result of alcoholism that the pain has made her willing to take suggestions. When an individual is so battered and beaten by her addiction, she no longer feels like fighting it, and this allows the new AA member to more willingly accept the First Step. Many of the women in this sample used this language. Some examples of remarks include: "Once I hit bottom, I knew I was powerless;" "when I hit bottom, I realized before I came into AA that I was powerless over alcohol;" and "Once I hit bottom, it was easy to see the reason why." Finally, some women in this sample who did not have any difficulty with the First Step not only willingly accepted their powerlessness over alcohol, but even derived a sense of release from giving up alcohol. Variations on the word "relief" appear in their comments. One woman "was relieved to discover alcohol and drugs were the root of my problems and that there was a place to go for help (AA)." Another recorded that, "It was a relief, actually, to find out I could be okay if only I didn't drink." Yet another woman echoed this same feeling. For her the release came, because "I thought that I was insane and was relieved to only be an alcoholic." These remarks illustrate the battle women are engaged in when they are drinking. The point is that women and men who come into AA feel as though they have been in a war zone with their addiction, and those who are beat up enough "surrender" more easily to the First Step of Alcoholics Anonymous.

The process of "surrendering" and admitting defeat in the battle against addiction is thought to be hastened, if the alcoholic has hit her bottom. In fact, hitting bottom expresses the sentiment felt by the early members of AA that one needed to exhaust all efforts to control alcohol by an exercise of will power, before that individual would be willing to try AA. Many early AA members believed that, if someone was not willing to accept her powerlessness over alcohol, she should "go back out" and drink until she had lost enough from various parts of her life (material possessions, relationships, jobs, physical or mental health, self-respect, or respect from others) to become willing to take the First Step. At the same time, however, the early members of AA also hoped—and they stated as much in the individual stories found in the Big Book—that alcoholics in the future would not have to experience the same kind of low bottoms that the early AA members experienced before they would try the AA program. In fact, another very popular AA saying reminds new members that "they can get off the elevator at any level; that they do not have to go to the basement." In this way, they are trying to encourage the suffering alcoholic to come into AA sooner rather than later. Today, it is much more common to hear AA members tell newcomers to "keep coming back," until they "get it," and the rougher edged advice to "go back out" is restricted to "hard core" AA types and for alcoholics who do not seem ready to surrender.

In summary, the women in this survey who believed they had hit their bottom had less difficulty with the First Step. These women were ready to give up the fight against their addiction and were more willing to accept the notion of powerlessness. On the other hand, women who did not think that they had hit bottom or who were still struggling with denial found the First Step more difficult. Those women who have relapsed, often several times, reported the First Step as being very difficult. Relapse is common among the women in this sample, as it is among recovering alcoholics in general, and denial is the primary psychological obstacle to surmount in order to work the First Step. Many alcoholics, including the women in this sample, do not want to give up on their own will power. Whatever the unmanageability in their lives, they still want to hold on to the illusion that they have control over their drinking. This is precisely what denial is. One woman reported that, "Even when I surrendered and accepted that I was an alcoholic it took me a while to understand that while I was drinking, booze had its way with me—I went on thinking that it gave me power and I had control over it." Another woman responded "I believed for a long time that I could control my drinking when it was clearly out of control." Yet another woman wrote, "Time in the program has allowed me to understand how destructive and devastating alcohol is for me. I need to respect that it can have power over me and can ruin me."

In addition to not wanting to give up the illusion that they could control their drinking by use of will power, some women still believed that alcoholism is a problem of discipline and lack of morality rather than a physiological and perhaps genetically-determined disease. As one woman put it "I thought sobriety was a moral issue and abstaining was merely a matter of will power and I had to learn that it is not a moral issue or a failure in life issue." Moreover, some women were ashamed

Table 4.1 Working Steps One & Three: Level of difficulty experienced by women in AA (percent)

Variable/Value	Women in AA
Level of Difficulty: Step 1	
Very difficult	32.0
Fairly difficult	13.5
Somewhat difficult	24.5
Not difficult at all	30.0
Total N	(162)
Level of Difficulty: Step 3	
Very difficult	27.5
Fairly difficult	26.0
Somewhat difficult	27.5
Not difficult at all	19.0
Total N	(153)

Note: Total number represents those women who have completed each step and responded to the question regarding that step.

of their addiction, not only because to them it signified inadequate will power, but also because they are women. For example, one woman wrote, "step one was difficult because 'good' women do not drink too much, much less become drunks." This sentiment mirrors what many women believe about alcoholism—that it is their own fault and that they should continue to try and control it. This thinking reinforces the effect of denial and makes it harder for some women to admit their powerlessness over alcohol.

The Second and Third Steps

The Second Step of AA reads, "Came to believe that a Power greater than ourselves could restore us to sanity." The Second Step introduces the idea that something outside of oneself is the source of recovery. Whereas the First Step identifies the problem, powerlessness over alcohol, the Second Step identifies the solution, a power greater than ourselves. The willingness to look for a power source in a spiritual direction and dimension is essentially what the Second Step requires. To complete this step, a woman needs to be open minded about the idea of looking toward something outside of self to help her recover from alcoholism.

The Third Step requires of the alcoholic a further extension in the spiritual direction. The language of the Third Step can give rise to misunderstandings. It reads, "Made a decision to turn our will and our lives over to the care of God *as we understood Him.*" The language is clearly Christian-influenced and gendered, referring to God as a "he." Beyond that, the language could lead one to think that AA requires cult-like submission from its members. As has been explained above, this is not the case. What the Third Step is intended to do is to arm the alcoholic for the sometimes difficult and painful work of the steps yet to come. Because the alcoholic has already been through a lot before getting to AA and has a myriad of problems coming into AA, it is too much to ask her to complete a moral inventory, admit her character flaws, and make amends to those she has harmed, if she has nothing to help her through this process. In AA, the reliance on a higher power is a substitute for what was once a dependency on alcohol. The Third Step asks the alcoholic to begin to develop a faith in her own, personally-defined divinity or higher power of whatever description. As described by elders in AA, the Third Step is nothing more than a decision to go and work the rest of the steps.

The language of AA is careful and deliberate in referring to "a power greater than ourselves" in the Second Step and to "God *as we understood Him*" in the Third Step. Bill Wilson and Dr. Bob both believed in the spiritual approach toward getting sober. Both also realized that traditional religious models would not work with alcoholics. From their own experience, they thought that alcoholics had to be introduced to the idea of spirituality rather than religion and that any mention of God had to be qualified. Hence, the Second Step merely introduces the idea of a "power greater than ourselves," and the Third Step reference to God is qualified by the clause *"as we understood Him."* (italics in the original) New members of AA are still handled gently, when it comes to what some AA members call "the God thing" or "the God issue." As reflected in the comments from the women participating in this research, this sensitivity is well placed, because many women do not easily turn their will over to God or any other higher power.

The term surrender is often used in AA meetings, and this word reflects the general consensus of recovering alcoholics of the past and of the present that giving all power to God is like throwing in the towel after a long battle. As was discussed in the analysis of the First Step, it is often only after an alcoholic has "hit bottom" or suffered enough pain or embarrassment that she will stop trying to control her obsession with alcohol. By making a decision to turn one's will over to the care of God as they understand him, alcoholics in AA are admitting that they cannot control their compulsion to drink. According to AA members, this initial act of turning their will over to God is an act of faith, a beginning belief that somehow, some way, the alcoholic can learn how to not drink and to live a happy and useful life.

As was true of the First Step, the majority of the women from this sample experienced some degree of difficulty with the Third Step. Approximately 77 percent fell into one of three levels of difficulty—somewhat, fairly, and very. Just under one-fifth of the women indicated no difficulty with this step (see table 4.1). It is probably worth restating that the italicized words *"as we understood Him,"* summarize the experience of the first members of AA. They do not bind any AA member to a set understanding of God, but rather they indicate that those first members each had to elaborate a personal understanding of God to which each of them individually had then been willing to turn over his or her alcohol problem. At times in AA this step is boiled down to the sentence, "You can't; God can; let Him." Despite the simplicity of the step, it is a significant action, especially for people who have been so accustomed to a relatively unrestricted use of their own will. And this is evidently why so many women in this survey had difficulty with it.

Eight out of every ten women participating in this survey had at least some difficulty working the Third Step. And the most salient explanation they provided to explain their difficulty is their resistance to turning their will and life over to a power greater than themselves, even one of their own understanding. Forty-one women provided narrative remarks, stating that the act of turning one's will over to a higher power is not an easy, finite, or definitive exercise. In fact, many of these women remarked that they have to work the Third Step every day, because they continue to struggle with "taking back" their own will. One woman exclaimed, "I have to work step three every day. Some days are easier than others. It's a tough concept to grasp especially for a control freak like me. I am still working on it, every day I have to remind myself that I am not in control." Many more women simply stated that they have to work on this step continually, because they persist in taking back their will. Some women remarked that the Third Step gets easier over time; yet others state that, even after twelve or thirteen years of sobriety, they still have to work on turning their will over.

This finding that women do not easily, simply, and unequivocally give up the use of their will power and turn their lives over to God is significant, given the concern among some feminists about AA. The first thing that it indicates is that these women are not comfortable turning their will and their lives "over to the care of God," even with the essential qualification *"as we understood Him."* (italics in the original) These women are not passive actors, seeking answers to their problems with alcohol and life by means of a blind surrender to something that will make all decisions for them. This finding is also interesting, because, if women are constantly struggling with surrendering their will, then they are not void of their own free will or the power to exercise their own will. This has been a concern of outsiders to AA and feminists who perceive AA as a totalizing environment, in which women are asked to admit that they are powerless and then are told to be dependent on God, and thus are unwittingly positioned into giving up their will.

The responses of the women in this survey about the Third Step reveal that for them not only is the action of the step not one of complete and mindless surrender of will, but in fact they determine for themselves the nature of the God with whom they attempt to engage as a result of this step. That is, they have not been told to turn their wills and lives over to a specific God, as defined by a specific religion or even by a particular religious culture. Rather, they themselves individually plot the characteristics of their own personal conceptions of God. For many, this understanding of God changed, as they worked the steps and as they built up more sober time. Therefore, the belief in God does not have to be absolute, complete, or all-inclusive. Indeed, an individual woman's faith may still be lacking or wavering, but she is not precluded from working the Third Step. In fact, an AA member can get sober and stay sober, while not fully trusting in God or God's will for her. This is an important finding, because it illustrates that the steps of AA are part of an ongoing process that is continuous and flexible and not definite or rigid. Moreover, the very fact that this step has been turned into a process by these women, when the language of the Third Step presents it as an event ("Made a decision . . ."), demonstrates that these women are working the Third Step in a manner that is comfortable to them. It may well be that one of the more fundamental differences between women and men in AA is this emphasis on process as opposed to a more typically male alcoholic's concern with event and task.

As the preceding discussion indicates, even when women admit that they are powerless over alcohol (the First Step), they do not automatically become susceptible to uncritical acceptance of pre-existing religious beliefs. Moreover, the experience of many of these women indicates that, even when a woman has begun to believe in a power greater than oneself, she does this cautiously, with a clear intent to understand her higher power and to turn her will over in contexts that she believes will help her. For example, many of the women who reported having a difficult time with the Third Step referred to having "control issues," and some stated that they are happiest, when they can turn their will over to God or a higher power. In the context of women in AA, the term "control issues" refers to an excessive need to exert control over "people, places, and things." That is, they are aware that in some instances attempting to control a situation only leads to more anxiety and to unrealistic expectations. This psychological need to control others and outside events is often discussed in AA, as well as in other twelve-step programs such as Adult Children of Alcoholics (ACA) and Al-Anon and in the community of professional alcohol counselors.

Control is a major issue in ACA. Many children who grow up in alcoholic environments often develop adaptive responses to help control or mitigate the dysfunctional circumstances created by the alcoholism of the adults in their lives. They attempt to control or direct events, because they are growing up in an environment that is uncertain, unpredictable and in some cases abusive. Similarly, many members of Al-Anon are spouses of alcoholics, who often adapt to the alcoholic in their lives by trying to control the environment. The selfishness and destruction that accompanies alcoholism places an inordinate and unhealthy burden of responsibility on children, spouses, and others, and, as a result, they develop excessive concerns with managing and directing circumstances that are really beyond their control. As a result of all of these considerations, this sample of women in AA revealed an orientation to the Third Step that made their surrender gradual and modulated, carefully defined and developed by the individual—even including her own personal understanding of the God to whom she was relinquishing some control—and involving processes that helped to establish a healthier psychological or spiritual balance, because the process of working the Third Step counteracted her obsessive quest for control.

For new members of AA, this can be confusing, because it can take a while for the woman to understand how she can have faith and still have use of her will. One woman who found the Third Step difficult admits, "I confused 'turning it over' to the care of a higher power with the handing responsibility of my children over." Feminist researchers have been concerned about this. Rapping (1996), for example, discusses a woman who appears to have turned everything over to a higher power without discretion. Despite the concerns of some feminist researchers, my read on the Third Step is that it is neither intended to create mindless followers of a specific religion or religious culture privileging males, nor does it inadvertently do so. The experiences of the women in this survey demonstrate that they defined the direction, pace, and extent of the spiritual or psychological processes connected with the Third Step.

This does not mean, as this discussion has already indicated, that these women encountered no difficulties in working this step. The biggest hurdles involved two issues: 1) developing trust in any God at all and 2) overcoming negative conceptions of God that precluded the development of the trust needed to work this step. In their open-ended responses, thirteen women stated that they not only have issues with letting go of control, but they also have trouble trusting a higher power or God. A couple of women offered explanations as to why they have difficulty trusting in God. One woman wrote, "I was unsure that this power really cared; also, I used to equate God with 'father'—as in my alcoholic father—and thus trust was slow to come." Another woman admitted that "I have always been skeptical about God because of the life I have had." The remainder of these thirteen women simply wrote that they had issues trusting God, a higher power, or anything outside of themselves.

Another thirteen women remarked that the Third Step was difficult mainly due to their preconceptions about religion and God. Ten of these women attributed their difficulty with the Third Step to their past religious experiences. They either did not receive any religious training in childhood, or they had come to reject the religious training of their childhood. For example, one woman shared that, "I was taught in childhood that you rely on yourself and God was never a part of my life." Another woman reflected that, "Growing up Catholic, I was very resistant to the higher power concept." A third woman was more specific and confided, "I had a hard time with the concept of God because I link my early religious upbringing with an older man who sexually abused me. I had to let go of any preconceived notions of a higher power before really doing the Third Step." A fourth woman admitted "I am an atheist and found it difficult to form a suitable concept." Still another woman stated, "My religion does not emphasize the Protestant symbols sometimes used in AA literature. The chapter in the Big Book, "We Agnostics," was extremely helpful." There was also one comment from a woman who confessed, "I do not like organized religion and had a really hard time separating religion from spirituality." Finally, one woman directly confronted the role of gender in her difficulty with the Third Step. She offered the explanation that, "As a woman I was constantly turning my life over to men and dysfunctional work dynamics. I claimed Goddess and still affirm feminine power." By whatever path, these women finally elaborated a vision of the divine that was approachable and supportive.

The very language of the Third Step—"Made a decision to turn our will and our lives over to the *care* of God" (author's italics)—denotes that the initial members of AA found it necessary to turn their wills over to a loving God. Looking at the remarks of the women in this survey who did not have any trouble with the Third Step, it is clear that most of them already had a conception of God or higher power that they were comfortable with. The remainder of the group who did not have difficulty with the Third Step were a handful of women who simply stated that they knew they needed help and were desperate enough to rely on a higher power, if that was what it took to stay sober. Except for a small minority who were already possessed of a belief in a loving God, the women in this survey did not come easily to the decision required by the Third Step. In addition to addressing the alcoholic problem of "self-will run riot," one of the major difficulties these women experienced with the Step was developing an understanding of religion, God, or spirituality to which they could turn their will over. Either way, the experiences these women describe do not support the feminists' concerns about this step.

Conclusion

It is clear that these women in AA value and take seriously the steps of AA. Their persistence in completing the steps demonstrates their commitment to working the Twelve Steps of the AA program, however difficult they may be. The first three steps of AA no doubt presented obstacles to recovery for these women. The First Step presented at least some difficulty for all but 30 percent of those who have completed it. The Third Step also challenged women, since all but 19 percent found the Third Step at least somewhat difficult. Notwithstanding these difficulties, the women in this sample overcame their struggles, wrestled with the language and potential implications of each step, and in the end allowed the steps to work as they were intended. Eventually, then, these three steps were transformed from obstacles into sources of support for recovery. In short, by completing the first three steps of AA, the women in this survey have begun to surrender to win.

5

Women Cleaning House: Steps Four through Nine

Once a woman has completed the first three steps, she has admitted her problem and has made a decision to seek an answer to that problem in AA by working the subsequent steps. Steps Four through Nine are considered the "housekeeping" steps of AA. As a woman approaches the Fourth Step, she is beginning the process of clearing away the wreckage of her past. She first identifies her character defects in the Fourth Step, openly admits these defects to God and another human being in the Fifth Step, asks God to remove these defects of character in the Sixth and Seventh Steps, and then identifies people she has harmed in the past and seeks to make amends for that harm in the Eighth and Ninth Steps. The intent of these steps is to remove barriers to living a spiritually-directed life as a way of overcoming the addiction to alcohol. This is the process of cleaning house. As stated in the so-called promises of AA, which are located in the "Big Book" directly after the discussion of the Ninth Step, "We are going to know a new freedom and a new happiness. We will not regret the past, nor wish to shut the door on it" (Alcoholics Anonymous 1976, 83).

As was stated in the preceding chapter, the participants in this study were asked to respond to a Likert scale about the difficulty they experienced in completing these steps. Once again, the steps will be introduced in a general way, and then the women's experiences with them will be analyzed, utilizing both quantitative and qualitative data.

The Fourth and Fifth Steps

The Fourth Step requires AA members to make "a searching and fearless moral inventory of ourselves." The so-called "Twelve and Twelve" book (Alcoholics Anonymous 1952) compares making a Fourth-Step inventory to the need that businesses have of taking periodic inventories. You look at what is stocked on the shelf and make note of what is there and what is needed. According to some of the AA members conversant with the steps, the inventory is intended to show the alcoholic exactly what drove her life, so as to prepare her to admit these shortcomings in the next step, to ready herself in the Sixth Step, and then to ask the God of her understanding to remove these defects in the Seventh Step. Once the alcoholic approaches Step Eight, she already knows who needs to go on her amends list to prepare her to go on to Step Nine and make amends. Therefore, the Fourth Step is essential to all of those steps that follow directly after it.

Once again, it is suggested to the alcoholic that this step and the others be taken, if she "wants what we have." That is, none of these steps are required for AA membership; that requirement is merely the desire to stop drinking. Many people in AA have been in "the rooms" for years without having formally worked the steps. Of this step, though, it is sometimes joked in AA meetings that "you don't have to work this step; you can do it when you come back in [after a relapse]." It is considered a vital stage of the process of spiritual awakening that leads the alcoholic into contact with a power greater than herself.

After this moral inventory has been taken, the alcoholic has a better understanding of the personal defects that have contributed to her compulsive and destructive behavior. She should now, according to AA, follow in the footsteps of the original AA members who stated that they had "Admitted to God, to ourselves, and to another human being the exact nature of our wrongs." This is the Fifth Step. The new AA member is to choose someone she trusts to tell her inventory to. Often this is her sponsor. Again, it is only a recommendation, and not a requirement, that the AA member work the steps. However, according to the Big Book, "If we skip this vital step, we may not overcome our drinking." (Alcoholics Anonymous 1976, 72). It can be heard in a step meeting of AA that the Fifth Step separates the girls from the women. By this, it is recognized that this is not an easy step to take and requires a lot of the new AA member. The following discussion addresses primarily the Fourth Step, since women were asked specifically about the level of difficulty they experienced with this step. However, the Fourth and Fifth Steps go hand-in-hand and many of the respondents address both in their narrative responses.

The Fourth Step of AA was, indeed, another difficult one for the women in this sample. Over 90 percent of those women who have completed the Fourth Step had difficulty with it. Roughly 30 percent of the women fell into one of three categories of difficulty—somewhat, fairly, and very difficult (see table 5.1). Fewer than one in ten of the women who have completed this step reported it as not being difficult at all.[1] Becoming willing to look at themselves honestly was the biggest barrier women in this survey had to overcome to work the Fourth Step.

Directly related to this, women reported having fear about what they would find out about themselves in working the Fourth Step. Feelings of shame and emotional pain were also frequently given as explanations for why the Fourth Step was difficult. It is very likely that few people would find taking a moral inventory of themselves to be a particularly easy or enjoyable task. For alcoholics who have caused a lot of moral harm by acts of omission or commission, even fewer embraced the task.

Table 5.1 Working Step Four: Level of difficulty experienced by women in AA (percent)

Variable/Value	Women in AA
Level of Difficulty: Step 4	
Very difficult	31.0
Fairly difficult	31.0
Somewhat difficult	28.5
Not difficult at all	9.5
Total N	(136)

Note: Total number represents those women who have completed Step Four and responded to the question regarding this step.

Many women specifically spoke to having difficulty with being honest with themselves about themselves. Some women simply stated that "It was hard to be honest." Other women expanded a little bit on their explanations. For example, one woman wrote, "It is hard facing the things I've done honestly." Another woman wrote, "It is hard to face the real me with feet of clay." One woman mentioned that "There was a lot I had been in denial about and didn't want to look at," and another woman exclaimed that "I found that being honest with/about me was a new experience." A couple of women expressed that the Fourth Step was difficult, because it required either an ability or willingness to look at meaningful information about themselves. For example, one woman wrote, "I had to look at issues which reveal deepest behavior patterns," and another woman admitted to purposeful forgetting, because "I was not able to see myself and my real feelings or motives." Still other women had difficulty, because they had a hard time accepting responsibility for their actions. For example, one woman reported that "It's hard to accept that my behavior led to other's behavior." Another woman reported that "It was hard to see myself and the negative impact that I have had upon my marriage." Yet, another woman simply stated "I couldn't look at myself and therefore I blamed others."

Several of the women who were afraid of being honest about themselves not only had difficulty completing the Fourth Step, but also took a long time to complete it. One woman wrote that it took her four years to complete this step, and another woman wrote that it took her five years to do the step with her sponsor. A third woman admitted that "It was difficult to look at myself after years of lying to myself about who I was. I was afraid there would be a lot of work... and there still is 8 years later." Finally, a fourth woman referred to a specific act that she was ashamed of that took her twelve years "to confess and try to understand."

Other women who had difficulty with the Fourth Step due to the challenge of being honest with and about themselves did not put off working the Fourth Step. They simply re-worked the step, until they felt that they had been rigorously honest. For example, one woman wrote, "My AA Forth Step is my third one. Now I'm down to the 'exact nature' of my wrongs which is very tough and elusive." Another woman wrote, "You see what you're ready to see at that point in time. When you do subsequent Forth Steps, you are able to go deeper." A third woman admitted that "The first one was hard; the next two were much easier. It was hard to see myself." A fourth woman exclaimed, "I did it three times looking for the perfect way. I really cleaned house, though." These women all wanted to work the Fourth Step diligently and did so, even if it meant re-working it until they got it right.

For other women in this sample, judging from their statements, fear was the greatest obstacle in completing this step. For example, several women simply disclosed in virtually identical terms that "I was very fearful to examine myself, or "I was fearful to look at myself," or finally "I was afraid of what I'd find." Another woman provided more detail and explained, "It was difficult to start the process out of fear of what "horrible" things I would find out about myself." Yet another respondent divulged, "I was afraid I was too self-centered and did not see things in the perspective I should have." All of these women revealed that the fear of learning about oneself made the Fourth Step difficult for them to complete.

In contrast to acknowledging fear before working the Fourth Step, one woman remembered that "I couldn't identify with self-centered fear in the Big Book, so I did this step using seven deadly sins. I have since recognized the role of fear." The self-centered fear that she referred to is not fear of the Fourth Step itself, but rather the fear that plays a prominent part in many alcoholics' lives. It is an emotion that many alcoholics have felt and lived with throughout their addiction. Self-centered fear is discussed at length in the Big Book in conjunction with the discussion of the Fourth Step. The Fourth Step discussion in the text Alcoholics Anonymous recommends a three-column balance sheet for alcoholics to use on their moral inventory. The first column is headed *"I'm resentful at."* The second reads *"The Cause."* And the third falls under the heading of *"Affects my."* Fear is listed as the cause in each instance of resentment (Alcoholics Anonymous 1976, 65). On the preceding page, resentment is referred to as the "number one" offender that "destroys more alcoholics than anything else (Alcoholics Anonymous 1976, 64)." So, according to AA, fear infuses almost every aspect of the alcoholic's life. Consequently, fear is often the topic of discussion in mixed meetings of AA.

In striking contrast to the prominence that self-centered fear has in AA's primary text and in mixed meetings, in the responses of the women in this survey it is practically non-existent. The specific mention that this one woman made of the absence of self-centered fear in her working of the Fourth Step corresponds to the absence of self-centered fear in the responses of the other women in this survey. The fear that they reference is the fear of looking at oneself in the context of working the Fourth Step. They have not, however, identified fear as something that permeated other areas of their lives. Instead, they have referred to honesty as the key component in working the Fourth Step. They have also provided some examples of where they need to be more honest in their lives and in looking at themselves. This is a very significant re-orientation of the Fourth Step on the part of these women. By substituting the concept of honesty and all that it implies for the role that fear has traditionally taken in working the Fourth Step of AA, these women have accomplished a substantial modification of the twelve-step recovery process.

Beyond the difficulty of being honest with themselves or of confronting their own fears of taking a moral inventory of themselves, the women in this sample provided other explanations as to why the Fourth Step was difficult. A few women said they had trouble identifying their faults or realizing "what their part" was in problems they had or things they had done. One woman wrote that "It was very hard to look at the part I played." Another echoed this reporting that "The hard part was seeing my part in the situations." A third expressed the same problem and identified the source of the difficulty, "It has been hard for me to see my part in my own life—because I was either emotionally numb or drinking." For a few other women, the main difficulties with the Fourth Step arose from feelings of shame. For example, one woman wrote, "I was resistance [sic] to honesty due to shame at actions and unwillingness to accept loss of control." Another woman wrote, "I was a shamed person with low self esteem." A third woman admitted she was ashamed of having an abortion. Another issue that gave several women difficulty was their aversion to the emotional pain it would cause. For example, one woman reported that, "It was painful to search that deep." Another woman acknowledged that, "It's hard to come to grips with emotional pain." Yet another woman admitted that "sitting down and writing such introspective and painful pieces from the past was something that elicited procrastination." Pain avoidance had a lot to do with the difficulty these women had in working the Fourth Step.

Lastly, several women are still trying to complete the Fourth Step and are having difficulty for all of the reasons just discussed. For example one woman wrote, "I've been stuck for several years . . . [because] of shame of my old behavior." Another woman reported, "It's hard to come to grips with emotional pain." A third woman answered with "The Forth Step is very humbling, I still have yet to disclose all to one person." A fourth woman shared that she is "still working on a thorough and complete inventory;" while a fifth woman stated that she is "having fear just thinking about doing it." It is because it is so difficult to undertake the painful review of the Fourth Step that AA encourages the alcoholic to first experience the surrender of the First Step, the hope inherent in the Second Step, and the act of faith in a loving God of the Third Step. The emotional scars, ravaged personal lives, and dysfunctional behavior that many alcoholics have experienced make this step a daunting prospect for most alcoholics, and for some it simply proves too difficult.

It appears that those few women, who did not find the Fourth Step difficult at all, were more accepting of themselves and of alcoholism as a disease, by the time they had come to their Fourth Step. For example, one woman explained, "By the time I did the 4th step I realized I had a disease and was sorry for hurt I had caused but it was a by-product of the disease—I had no control over it." Another woman simply felt ready to confront herself and her alcoholism. This woman recounted that, "I wanted to right my life for myself and my husband and children. I had to be honest to myself and family and face reality." A third woman addressed the technical aspect of writing the step, but also admitted that she was emotionally ready to work the step. This respondent stated "I'm a writer by trade so writing was not difficult. Also, I was ready to stop hurting." A final comment was provided by a woman who also appeared ready to work this step, although she suggests that her readiness came slowly and not so deliberately. This woman replied, "It came gradually and naturally. I didn't work it so much as much as it worked me while life was happening." Members of AA often refer to a step "working them" rather than them working the step. By framing their experience in these terms, AA members and this woman in particular, are expressing their belief that, if one is open-minded, willing, and actively engaged in the recovery process, then eventually she will have worked all Twelve Steps of AA. According to this understanding of the experience, the member must in a general way be cognizant, disciplined and engaged, but that the process does not have to be burdensome or painful. There are many other slogans heard in AA, such as, "easy does it," "AA is the easier softer way," and "wear AA like a loose garment"—that can be seen as favoring a lighter and less onerous interpretation of AA and the Twelve Steps. Whatever the rationale and for whatever reason, not everyone found the Fourth Step to be such a burdensome process, although the vast majority of these women were not able to take the Fourth Step in such an easy stride.

Another approach toward the Fourth Step that professionals from the treatment community have encouraged among women (Beattie 1987; Covington 1982) is the inclusion of a list of character assets, as well as character defects, in the moral inventory. Many professionals in the treatment community feel that women come into AA weighed down with poor self-esteem, shame, and guilt and therefore women should not work the Twelve Steps in a manner that will reinforce these negative emotions. Therefore, they have suggested that women look at their strengths and not just their weaknesses in working the Fourth Step. Whether this adaptation came completely from treatment professionals or also developed independently among women in AA, it seems to have permeated the ranks of women in AA, because almost all the women in this survey who included assets on their Fourth Step inventory list did so at the suggestion of their sponsors. Almost three-fourths of the women in this survey who have completed the Fourth Step reported that they had made an inventory of their character assets, too, as part of the Fourth Step. The way that the women in this sample have modified the execution of the Fourth Step too is similar to the way that they transformed the Third Step into more of a process than an event, even accommodating multiple workings of the step. The insignificant role attributed to self-centered fear, the absence of resentment as an issue in these women's narratives and the widespread adoption of a gentler approach to their moral inventories indicate that these women in AA are indeed working the steps from their own gendered perspective and not that of the dominant group—men.

Before leaving the Fourth Step, it is worth noting that some women identified more positive aspects of this stage of the recovery process. For at least a couple of women, the process of getting past the fear and the emotional pain that the Fourth Step held for them actually resulted in a great feeling of relief. One woman exclaimed, "Great step for me once I got over the fear that it would make me drink; it was a relief to be so honest with myself." A second woman wrote "I was thorough and detailed and tried to capture all the ugliness and craziness. The picture that emerged was painful, but finally I understood how alcohol f—up most of it. There was finally an explanation." The common saying has it that "no pain, no gain." For most of these women there had been plenty of pain, but it was never accompanied by any real gain, just more alcoholic destructiveness. At least the pain of the Fourth Step brought with it a great sense of relief and the prospect of self-respect.

The Sixth and Seventh Steps

Step Six reads, "Were entirely ready to have God remove all these defects of character," and Step Seven reads, "Humbly asked Him to remove our shortcomings." After the Fifth Step, the Sixth and Seventh Steps are taken in rapid succession. The Sixth Step is supposed to be done immediately after the Fifth, and the alcoholic is advised to take some time by herself, that is a few hours, to reflect on what she has just done. This moves her on to the Sixth and Seventh Steps.

Participants in this survey were asked what other steps had been difficult for them, and several women responded that the Sixth and Seventh were difficult. Character defects are thought to be maladaptive behaviors an alcoholic has acquired, learned or simply exaggerated as a result of her addiction. Some view these "defects of character" as moral imperfections in one's character, for others character defects are perceived to be "defense mechanisms" used to cope with the abnormality of the alcoholic life. Whatever one's view, the Sixth and Seventh Steps require the recovering woman to identify her character flaws and then ask God to remove them. One woman underestimated the demands of these steps. In her words, "The compulsion to drink lifted immediately when I turned to AA for help and I was expecting an equally speedy recovery from my other character defects." But, for the most part, the reasons that these women struggled with these steps can be broken down into two categories: 1) a reluctance to look at themselves honestly and then be willing to surrender the shortcomings they identified, 2) a greater emphasis on process than outcome. The way in which these women worked the Sixth and Seventh Steps demonstrate some continuities and similarities with how they worked the Third and Fourth Steps, especially the emphasis they put on process and the resistance they felt to looking at themselves. Their narratives make clear that these steps, too, were worked in a style that fit them and made them, if not comfortable, then at least less uncomfortable.

In the analysis of the experience these women had with the Fourth Step, it became clear that the source of difficulty for many of them was their hesitation at examining themselves and their past behaviors. The shame, embarrassment or disappointment that they felt at the prospect of a rigorous self-examination played a far more prominent part in their experiences with the Fourth Step than did the resentment and self-centered fear emphasized in the presentation of the Fourth and Fifth Steps in the text *Alcoholics Anonymous*. Those same motivations and feelings reveal themselves in the comments these women made about their Sixth and Seventh Steps. For example, one woman admitted, "It is hard to identify some of my defects—not entirely ready to let go of them—still in denial about some shortcomings." Another woman exclaimed, "The ability to change, even when wanted, is hard to do." A third woman disclosed, "I took a long time to become willing to let go of some character defects—some that were masquerading as assets in my mind." Another woman shared, "Becoming ready to remove character defects is difficult; I usually become more ready when it becomes evident that holding on to defects perpetuates the pain I want to be free of." One woman explained, "One's defects are familiar; and it is a real struggle to let go of part of oneself." Another woman echoed the same sentiment, "Some defects I feel painfully comfortable with." A third woman replied, "It's hard to give up character defects that work so well for you." There is an undertone of fear of change in these comments that comes out clearly in the statements of a couple of the women. One woman expressed a real fear of the steps. She communicated that, "Having started therapy fifteen years before recovery, I was afraid of the person that I had been becoming." Perhaps the way that one woman expressed her experience with these steps captured best the overall orientation of these women to the Sixth and Seventh Steps. She reported that:

> I can today see with more clarity my character defects—such as low self-esteem, arrogance, self-righteousness, and people-pleasing—

which lead [sic] me to working the Sixth and Seventh Steps—
becoming willing to have these defects removed, and asking God to
remove them. I struggled with these steps, too, because I feared if I
prayed for God to remove my shortcomings, there would be nothing
left of me!

Fear of change and fear of what they would see about themselves
expressed itself in the experiences of many women in this group, as they
worked the Sixth and Seventh Steps, getting transformed into a general
reluctance to work the steps.

For other women, the Sixth and Seventh Steps took on aspects of a
protracted process not unlike their approach to the Third Step. One
woman confided, "I've been on them a long time—two years. I am just
beginning to clearly see my character defects." Another woman
reported, "I easily lose track of my character defects—and these two
steps require sustained effort." Finally, another woman provided a quick
summary of her experience, "I've since come to accept this is a lifetime
process. As I have experienced this step, it is not as easy as it sounds.
You can be pretty attached to your defects. Your head tells you to get rid
of them. Your heart says, well, I'm kind of used to this one or that one. I
find myself working on this one pretty much all the time." Like the
approach many women in this group adopted in relation to the Third
Step, a significant proportion of these women defined their approach to
the Sixth and Seventh Steps, too. Rejecting the speedy, event-oriented
treatment provided in the Big Book, these women made of the Sixth and
Seventh Steps an experience and a set of tools for a longer, more
thorough self-examination and transformation.

The Eighth and Ninth Steps

The Eighth Step of AA reads, "Made a list of all persons we had
harmed, and became willing to make amends to them all." The Eighth
Step consists of two distinct tasks, making a list of the people who have
been harmed by the alcoholic and then being "willing to make amends
to them all." This is not always an easy or quick task, because many of
the people who have been harmed by alcoholics have also harmed the
alcoholics themselves. So, according to the Big Book, there is often a
process of forgiveness that must occur for this step to be successful.
Some alcoholics have found great release in this forgiveness, especially
when the individual in question is someone very close to the alcoholic.
Once that willingness is present, the alcoholic can go on to the Ninth

Step and make "direct amends to such people wherever possible, except when to do so would injure them or others."

The Eight Step does not appear to have been a very difficult or even a fairly difficult step for the majority of the women in this sample who have done it. Over forty percent of those women who have worked this step did not find it difficult at all, and a third found the step only somewhat difficult (see table 5.2). In contrast to the high degree of difficulty experienced on some of the other steps, less than a quarter of those women who had completed this step found it to be either fairly or very difficult, and only seven percent found it very difficult to do the Eighth Step.[2] Although these women do not report great difficulty with this step, it appears here too that they adapted the process in completing this step.

Table 5.2 Working Step Eight: Level of difficulty experienced by women in AA (percent)

Variable/Value	Women in AA
Level of Difficulty: Step 8	
Very difficult	7.3
Fairly difficult	17.4
Somewhat difficult	33.1
Not difficult at all	42.2
Total N	(109)

Note: Total number represents those women who have completed Step 8 and responded to the question regarding this step.

As was true of the way they worked the Fourth Step, many of these women have slightly modified the Eighth Step in the way that accommodates their specific needs. For example, some of the women include a list of those who have harmed them, in addition to making a list of those they have harmed. More than a fourth of the women in this sample have done this. Another, simpler way used to adapt the step was to add themselves to the list of people they had harmed. In this way, the women were acknowledging their need to exercise forgiveness toward themselves, as well as asking forgiveness of others for damaging actions they had committed while they were active alcoholics. For many women, recognizing and then accepting that alcoholism is a disease allows them for the first time to let go of some of the shame and guilt that they have acquired over their drinking lives. Similarly, I heard in several of the women's meetings that their healing does not really begin until they forgive themselves first and then they can move onto forgiving others.

AA literature and practice emphasizes that in the Eighth and Ninth Steps alcoholics need only be concerned with "cleaning up your side of the street." In that regard, making a separate list of those who have done harm to the alcoholic strays from the intent of the step, as envisioned by the first, mostly male members of AA and by AA at present, which is still two-thirds male. Evidently, many women in AA carry a more burdensome sense of shame and guilt, so that the special adaptations of the Eighth Step discussed in this section prove very beneficial as a means of lightening that burden of shame.

As has been noted, a significant proportion of the women in this study who had worked the Eighth Step did not find it difficult to any significant degree. The most common response from women who did not find the Eighth Step difficult came from respondents who stated that making the list itself was not difficult. In a majority of these cases, the women noted that their Fourth Step had already outlined who should be on their Eighth-Step list. Others declared that it was easy to make an Eighth-Step list, because it was obvious or clear to them who should be on the list. In another instance, the respondent indicated that her sponsor helped her identify who should be on the Eighth-Step list. For all of these respondents, the point of concern was technical aspects of completing the task rather than any emotional issues related to working the Eighth Step.

A few others explained that the Eighth Step was not difficult, because they were so primed for it. One woman stated that, "I was emotionally ready." Another was relieved to be at this stage. She indicated that "I always felt I wronged everyone and wanted to apologize." Or, as another woman put it simply and directly, "It was a relief to make amends."

For several other women the Eighth Step did not prove difficult because, according to their narrative responses, their drinking hurt mostly family members and others close to them. A few women summarized themselves as "at home drunks," so that they harmed only those they lived with. In one instance, the woman's list included only family members, all of whom were deceased by the time she did her Eighth Step. This respondent noted that, "Since I drank at home mainly, the people I had harmed were family members, particularly my mother and husband, who are deceased." Other women acknowledged this same painful truth: that the people hurt most by their drinking were the people close to them. One stated simply "I harmed my family." Another admitted that "I know I harmed my husband and children, there was no one else." Another extended the circle a bit, but it still contained only those with close connections to her: "I was an isolated drunk—those I harmed most were close family members, an employer, and a few friends." Another woman did not report the Eighth Step as difficult, but she admitted, "It took a while for me to realize how much I had negatively affected my husband." Interestingly, only one woman out of those who found the Eighth Step not difficult included herself on her Eighth Step list. In addition to those people close to her, this respondent recounted that, "I felt that I was the one who had been most harmed and only immediate family members were on my list."

For those women who did find the Eighth Step difficult, the majority did not want to admit the harm they had done to others or experience the pain associated with harming others. Their answers reveal the pain they felt over having behaved in such destructive fashion. One woman said that it was "hard to accept harm done to others." Another reported that it was, "difficult to be honest about whom I had harmed." One woman admitted that, "I was afraid to look within," while another woman replied that "realizing my part in past problems was hardest with close family (husband) and children." A few women communicated that it was experiencing emotional pain that made this step difficult. For example, one woman revealed that it was "more difficult to come to terms with pain I caused others, especially those close to me," and another respondent wrote that the step "requires going over painful times in your life." What it all came down to, according to one woman, is the fact that, "the list was painful to make."

In addition to not wanting to recognize the harm done to others or to revisit painful experiences, a few women found that their own harsh judgment of themselves made the Eighth Step difficult. For example, one respondent shared, "I thought admitting I was wrong equated to being a bad person, at first." A second woman disclosed that she still has feelings of guilt associated with her parents, because, as she confided, "one of them (father) molested me for many years—it led to therapy and I am not in his life right now, it is healthier to stay away." A third woman noted "I have been paralyzed by fear that the 'blame' for all my wrongs lies entirely on me when I know I've suffered extreme Post Traumatic Stress Disorder that flattens me." Similarly, two other women expressed difficulty being willing to make amends to people who had

·harmed them. The first woman stated, "I didn't want to count the ones who'd harmed me," and the second woman more or less faulted herself for feeling that "I have always felt sensitive to pain others inflicted on me or I perceived had been inflicted on me." In all these cases, the Eighth Step was perceived as difficult due to the respondent's own tendency toward excessive self-blame.

In summary, women in this sample who have completed the Eighth Step of AA have generally not had difficulty with this step. They interpreted the step as easy, because they could identify the people who should be on the list and focused on only those closest to them. When identifying those they had harmed, many women reported that they were "at home drunks" and therefore their drinking affected mostly their immediate family members. For those women who did find the Eighth Step difficult, it was because they did not want to look at the harm they had caused others or because they did not want to revisit the pain associated with harming others. Similarly, a handful of women expressed guilt and self-blame for harm that was done to them.

Between those who made a list of people who had harmed them and those who added themselves to the list of people owed amends, more than a third of the women in this survey who had done the Eighth Step had adapted it in some way to fit a more specifically female gendered paradigm. Given that some researchers (Beattie 1987; Covington 1982) encouraged women to add themselves to amends lists and that it is a frequent topic of discussion at women-only step meetings, it is perhaps surprising that the percentage is as low as it is. In this regard, it is revealing that only a couple of women who provided narrative responses in this survey even spoke of looking at those who had harmed them or even of adding themselves to their amends list. The experiences of these women on a relatively straightforward step such as the Eighth Step reveal a great deal about women in AA. First of all, these findings indicate that women in this survey and perhaps in AA at large do not express points of view consistent with a victim mentality. On the contrary, women work the Eighth Step more traditionally than what might have been expected and take on the full responsibility for their actions, at least as represented in the amends lists that they make. At the same time, the women in this survey actively adapted the Eighth Step to respond to the greater sense of shame, blame and self-recrimination that women alcoholics seem to feel compared to male alcoholics. As has been seen in the discussion of the other steps, women in this sample are not passive receptors of male-structured recovery systems, nor are they reconfiguring AA's steps to accommodate a victim mentality. Rather they are assuming responsibility for their own recovery in a proactive, creative, and gendered fashion.

Before leaving this discussion about Steps Four through Nine, I would like to make one more mention of the role of forgiveness implicit in these steps. For those women who have experienced severe abuse at the hands of another, forgiveness does not come easily, especially in the aftermath of reliving much of the pain incumbent when working the Fourth and Fifth steps. However, the traditional essence of forgiveness allows a woman to free herself of the "wreckage of the past," even when it is no fault of her own. Because this is a touchy area from a feminist point of view, many might want to exclaim "Why ask women to victimize themselves again or why not take a more proactive stance toward abusers?" The response is better left to the words of those in recovery and how they understand the benefits of working these steps. A woman who had a past experience of incest (noted in a previous chapter) and who had blamed her mother all of her life for not intervening writes "It took three fourth and fifth steps before I was able to make peace with my mother, make my amends, and have a real relationship with her for six years before she died. My father was dead for sixteen years by the time I got sober, but I have made peace with him too, through the steps of AA." In this tragic story, it was not so much anger at the primary perpetrator but the missed relationship with the mother that haunts this woman. As she tells it, "until her death, at age 78, she always denied knowing anything about the activities between me and my father and today I realize that this may be true." So, for this woman these steps were indeed freeing.

Conclusion

Women in AA clean up the wreckage of their past by working steps Four through Nine. Most of the women who have completed the Fourth Step had at least some difficulty with the step. These women attribute their difficulty to their fear of being honest with themselves. This fear is slightly different from the fear described in the main text of AA, which describes the alcoholic's fear as based on self-centeredness. The reluctance to look at one's self honestly continues to cause some difficulty for women in working steps Five through Seven. Women identify feelings of shame and embarrassment as hurdles to overcome in completing these housecleaning steps. However, by the time these women get to the Eighth and Ninth Steps, they are acutely aware of their character flaws and shortcomings and are willing to make amends to themselves and others. Given their lack of difficulty in working Step

Eight, it is clear that these women no longer struggle with being honest with themselves and in fact have come to forgive themselves. The emphasis on honesty and forgiveness in relationship to themselves as well as others demonstrates that women in AA indeed work the steps as recommended, but they do so in a fashion consistent with their own gendered interpretation and practice of Steps Four through Nine.

Notes

[1] Thirty-one women out of a sample size of 167 had not completed the Fourth Step.

[2] Fifty-eight out of 167 women had not worked the Eighth Step.

6

Women Passing It On: Steps Ten through Twelve

In AA, Steps Ten through Twelve are considered the growth and maintenance steps. These steps are worked on a continuous basis and help the alcoholic develop her spiritual condition. The Tenth Step is a very practical step and simply asks the AA member to take a daily inventory, an abbreviated Fourth Step, and to promptly admit her wrongs (an abbreviated Fifth Step). By doing so, the AA member continues to keep her house in order and frees herself up to develop her conscious contact with God or a higher power, as she is instructed to do in Step Eleven. Finally, after completing all of the previous steps, a woman now has what AA terms "a spiritual awakening" and in turn she is asked to help other alcoholics. At this point, especially when an experienced member of AA works with another female alcoholic who is just starting to get sober by working the steps, the cycle of recovery is repeated. In AA this is often called "passing it on."

The Tenth and Eleventh Steps

The Tenth Step, "Continued to take personal inventory and when we were wrong promptly admitted it," instructs the recovering alcoholic to be mindful of her transgressions against other people and to carry herself with dignity and respect. As in the Eighth Step, women do not have to admit wrongs where it is not warranted, but they simply need to recognize, if they have acted against their own newly-defined code of conduct. As the Big Book puts it, "We should be sensible, tactful, considerate and humble without being servile or scraping. As God's people we stand on our feet; we don't crawl before anyone." (Alcoholics Anonymous 1976, 83) The key thing that the alcoholic accomplishes through this step is to stay vigilant in looking for any signs of old character defects, the most traditional being selfishness, dishonesty, resentment, and fear. However, as noted in the previous steps, women may include other defects of character that pertain more to their own gendered situation. This can include not letting others walk over them, or, as it was stated by a woman in one of the meetings attended for this research project, "I have to not let myself be a doormat." Women also address the more traditional aspects of selfishness, as described in the Big Book, but they are more likely to describe their unbecoming behaviors as indulging in self-pity or throwing temper tantrums. Throughout the course of the day, the Tenth Step allows for self-correction and minimization of old, so-called "alcoholic" behaviors. As is the case with the other steps, they apply the Tenth Step in ways that address their own specific needs as women.

The Eleventh Step reads, "Sought through prayer and meditation to improve our conscious contact with God *as we understood Him*, praying only for knowledge of His will for us and the power to carry that out." The Big Book emphasizes the idea that alcoholics have a "daily reprieve" from alcoholism and that the reprieve is contingent on keeping spiritually grounded. The Eleventh Step fulfills that function in sobriety. Since the women in this survey have shown the capacity to devise adaptations to the steps preceding this one, it would seem likely that alternative forms of spirituality might express themselves in the experiences of women alcoholics, too. While that is probably the case, it is also true that the most popular and frequently used means of maintaining "conscious contact" and a sound spiritual foundation among these women are the traditional means suggested by AA.

The women in this sample were asked to check all activities that they participate in as part of working the Eleventh Step. Nearly all of the women, over 95 percent who have reached the Eleventh Step, listed regular attendance at AA meetings as one of their spiritual tools.[1] The second most frequently engaged in spiritual practice was prayer, which was reported by 86 percent of the women in that sample.[2] Only one other spiritual exercise is practiced on a regular basis by substantially more than half the women in this survey, and that is reading AA literature (Conference-approved books, articles, and pamphlets), which was checked on over three-fourths of the surveys (see table 6.1). A handful of these women specifically mentioned that they work with, talk to, have fellowship with, and sponsor other AA members to help them develop their conscious contact with God. In short, the practices engaged in by the largest number of these women are centered in the heart of the traditional AA program: meetings, prayers, and AA literature. This is a somewhat surprising finding, given the propensity these women have shown to adapt AA's culture to the profile of their needs.

However, it is not as if these women do not engage in spiritual practices of a less traditional kind. Just over half of the women who had completed this step practice yoga or other forms of meditation. Five women remarked that they read spiritual literature or listen to meditations on tapes. Another five women engage in some form of exercise such as walking, running, lifting weights, aerobics and Tai Kwon Do. Four women mentioned writing in a journal on a regular basis. Three women consider involvement with nature a spiritual activity. One of them remarked that, "Gardening is prayer and meditation for me." Two other women take nature walks on a regular basis. In addition, six women report being involved in other spiritual programs. Two women have taken "A Course in Miracles." Two women have spiritual directors to guide their exercises and practices, and one woman is a certified spiritual director.[3] Another woman had participated in transcendental meditation (TM), and another mentioned Native American spirituality. Over a quarter of these women have either attended workshops on personal healing related to spirituality or have participated in non-church based spiritual programs outside of AA. These women have a rich and diverse range of spiritual practices.

No matter what the means, the women in this sample are active in working the Eleventh Step. It is clear, as measured on two different questions in this survey, that the spiritual program of the women in this sample is grounded first and foremost in AA. They regularly attend AA meetings to keep their God consciousness at a high level, and they supplement AA meetings with prayer and readings from AA literature. These are the practices of the overwhelming majority of these women. Many attempt to work this step on a daily and ongoing basis. For example, one woman wrote, "I meditate most days in the morning and evening and give my day some thought after meditation." Another woman shared that:

> This step is like breathing. It is a daily exercise. I put it aside, maybe, when I go to a Mel Gibson movie and I am just relaxing in the moment, but I am aware of working this step all the time. In practice, I try to do the next right thing, every moment of every day. When I don't feel like doing it, I take a nap or go to the movies.

A good proportion of this group also engages in non-AA spiritual programs, some of which are not part of the Western and traditional American religious heritages. But these are clearly secondary and supplemental to their AA-based spiritual exercises. Since this group of women has not hesitated to adapt AA culture by means of women-only meetings and specific changes to the core of AA—that is, the steps—then it is safe to assume that, if AA's religious culture constrained or hindered their spiritual development and spiritual condition, these women would be more active in either adapting AA's spiritual culture or in seeking religious alternatives outside AA. It appears that AA's non-denominational, big tent, "God *as we understood Him*" spiritual culture is not so male-dominated and traditional as to constitute an obstacle to the sobriety of this group of recovering women alcoholics.

Table 6.1 Summary of Eleventh- & Twelfth-Step activities engaged in by women in AA (percent)

Variable/Value	Women in AA
Eleventh Step (top three activities)	
Regular attendance to AA meetings	95.5
Prayer	86.0
Reading AA literature	77.6
Total N	(112)
Twelfth Step (top three activities)	
Assist in meeting functions	91.0
Hold group positions	79.2
Sponsorship	74.0
Total N	(101)

Notes: Respondents were not limited to one response only. The survey instrument was modified after the first 25 surveys to include new categories under the Eleventh and Twelfth Steps. The categories of "prayer" under the Eleventh Step and "sponsorship" under the Twelfth Step include a sample frame of 93 and 100, respectively.

The Twelfth Step

The Twelfth Step reads "Having had a spiritual awakening as the result of these steps, we tried to carry this message to alcoholics, and to practice these principles in all our affairs." The Twelfth Step of AA links the alcoholic back to the world with a service orientation. The two parts of the step—helping other alcoholics and practicing these principles in all our affairs—are actually variations on the same theme of service. The principles referred to are the spiritual principles practiced in the preceding steps: principles such as honesty, humility, forgiveness, gratitude and so on. The most specific way that these principles are to be applied is through helping other alcoholics. This is what AA members refer to as "Twelfth-Step work." It is important to understand that this step is neither an afterthought nor a completion of the steps. Rather, continuing Twelfth-Step work is the key to maintaining sobriety, and, as such, it receives a lot of attention in AA. It is the "primary purpose" cited in the Fifth Tradition,[4] and it is also the way that an established AA member stays sober. By working with other alcoholics, especially newcomers, the established AA member "keeps it green," reminding her of what it was like for her when she drank, thereby counteracting the alcoholic tendency to forget the negative aspects of drinking and to romanticize it. In addition, by getting the alcoholic "out of herself" to work effectively with a newly sober alcoholic, the Twelfth Step helps alleviate the primary spiritual and personality disorder of alcoholics, according to AA, selfishness. In all these ways, the Twelfth Step is intended to be the practical outcome of the spiritual awakening that the AA member has had as a direct result of working the steps.

Questions about Twelfth-Step work were put to the women in this survey as a means of gauging their participation in the service work of AA. The questions involved a range of Twelfth-Step activities, including assisting in meeting functions, holding a group position, sponsoring other members, taking an alcoholic to a detox center or a hospital, answering the phone at a local intergroup office, serving as a General Service Representative (GSR), and other similar activities. Many of these are activities members can engage in before they have actually completed the eleven preceding steps. For example, newly sober women have given rides to meetings to women who are living in a rehabilitation home or hospital. Other women held a group position, such as being the coffee maker or being a secretary for a meeting. These service positions are one means of making the newly-sober alcoholic feel a part of AA from the very outset. In addition, certain types of Twelfth-Step work involve responsibilities that are central to the viability of both the groups and of AA as a whole. Hence, Twelfth-Step activities constitute a crucial litmus test of members' incorporation into AA culture and of their "sense of ownership," so to speak, of AA.

The women in this sample have performed the full range of Twelfth-Step activities.[5] The most common activity found in this sample of AA members is helping out with the operations of an AA meeting. To illustrate, nine out of ten women who had gotten to the Twelfth Step had assisted in meeting functions such as setting up chairs, making coffee, and cleaning up. Almost eight out of ten had held a group position of some responsibility such as secretary, treasurer, or literature person. Just shy of three-quarters of these women have sponsored other AA members.[6] Over 40 percent have taken an AA meeting to a treatment facility, rehabilitation center, hospital, or correctional facility. Smaller, but still significant percentages of the women surveyed have performed other essential services such as taking an alcoholic to a detox center or treatment facility and answering phones at an intergroup office to give general guidance to people calling AA for help (see table 6.1).

The most significant and dramatic finding relative to women alcoholics and Twelfth-Step work is the fact that over one-fifth of these women have served as a General Service Representative (GSR). Since the GSR represents her group at local and area conventions or meetings, at which general issues affecting AA are discussed, this is a very responsible position within AA. Unlike many of the other positions, such as coffee maker or group secretary, GSRs are individuals who have some time in sobriety and who are trusted by their groups. It is also a position that a woman could refuse with more justification in the eyes of other AA members, than, say, a secretary position. Women are being chosen for these positions and are accepting the responsibility. The high rate of participation recorded by the women in this survey indicates that they are completely integrated into AA. Comparable figures for male AA members are not available, but almost 21 percent is a very high proportion. In sum, there are no AA service functions that these women have not been involved with, and they are overrepresented in the one service function that indicates a substantially higher degree of integration and trust. Once again, the experience of these women with the Twelfth Step confirms the other evidence cited to the effect that women are fully and actively engaged in their recovery and in AA.

This section of the survey provides a clear sense of the variety, range and number of Twelfth-Step activities these women are involved in. In addition to the activities discussed in the preceding paragraph, numerous other activities were reported by almost a quarter of the women who had completed the first eleven steps. Many of these other activities involved working with newcomers: driving them to meetings, talking with them, giving a newcomer their phone numbers and encouraging them to call, and generally being available to them. Another group of activities involved tasks related to the functioning of an AA meeting or AA organization. Examples include getting speakers for meetings, working the AA hotline, working at an AA club, starting new meetings, editing a newsletter, and serving in leadership roles. A few women specifically stated that they try to "practice these principles in all my affairs," referring to the second part of the Twelfth Step. Four other women are professionals in the field of addictions recovery, such as working in a detox or rehabilitation facility. In two cases, women have organized new groups to bring meetings to sick AA members, one in a hospital and another confined to her home. Another woman developed an educational program for older people to encourage senior centers to allow AA meetings on their grounds. Finally, one woman listed many non-AA volunteer activities and organizations that she has become involved in, including a suicide hot line, a rape hot line, "Parents Supporting Parents," "On Our Own," and the "National Alliance of the Mentally Ill."

Overall, women in this sample have been very active members in AA. The activities related to the operation of an AA meeting and the organization of AA require varying levels of responsibility and commitment. For example, an AA member who agrees to make coffee for a particular meeting has to attend every week (or arrange for someone to fill in) and has to arrive early enough to have the coffee ready when people start arriving for the meeting. Other functions of an AA meeting, such as being the group secretary, involve somewhat greater responsibility. Many AA groups require an AA member to have a specified length of sobriety, such as six months or a year, before she is eligible to be secretary, because this position is important to the smooth operations of the meeting. The women in this survey have been involved in the full range of such essential AA activities.

The Twelfth Step and Sponsorship

The most personal and intensive type of Twelfth-Step work is sponsorship. There is no requirement that a member of AA have a sponsor, but the sponsorship relationship is essentially what Bill Wilson and Dr. Bob Smith discovered to be the key to staying sober: active work with another alcoholic in order to lead a spiritual life based on service. The overwhelming majority of people who come to AA have been worked over pretty well by the chaos of their lives. They are vulnerable, uncertain, and confused. The culture, language, and practices of AA are more or less foreign to them. In these circumstances, a sponsor can be a very important person in the newcomer's life. The sponsor initially helps the newcomer understand the language and the steps of AA and answers general questions about AA. Ultimately, the sponsor helps to guide a new member of AA through the Twelve Steps and in so doing often builds a personal relationship with the newcomer.

It is clear that the women in this sample of AA members do indeed value the role of sponsorship. Fully three-quarters of the women in this sample who have completed the Twelfth Step have sponsored other alcoholic women. Conversely, 78 percent of the total sample of women in this survey have a sponsor. This statistic is consistent with the figures reported in AA's most recent membership survey conducted in 2004.[7] Sponsorship is yet another example of how these women are fully incorporated into AA.

The vast majority of the women in this survey speak highly of sponsorship. They believe having a sponsor was crucial to their getting and staying sober in AA. The extensive comments of one woman about her first sponsor, Louise, are indicative of the profound attachment and spiritual or psychological connection AA members feel toward their sponsors. Sponsorship relationships vary, and each AA member defines for herself the role she is willing to play in another AA member's life. The point of this extended passage is not that Louise is a "typical" sponsor. Rather, the passage imparts a sense of the significance and intimacy of the sponsorship relationship. This woman wrote of her sponsor:

> Her name was Louise, she was a former top Sergeant in the army and as tough as nails and she saved my life. She assigned several books for me to read daily, call her daily, attend 90 meetings in 90 days, ask God for help staying sober this day every morning and 'Thank Him' for a day's sobriety every night. Louise also told me every day that God loved me and that I was where he wanted me to be. I knew this was true because Louise had a good connection to God. I had lost touch with the God whom I had grown up with some years before when I started drinking, because I knew that it was wrong. When the tragedies happened I had cursed God and knew that He had forgotten me and was punishing my whole family because I had been so bad. Boy I had all the delusions of grander [sic] in the book but little by little I got better. Louise had me reading the 1st step for the first month, and the 1st, 2nd and 3rd steps daily. She would ask me what I thought about, what I had read and we would discuss any questions I had. It is my belief that God puts people into our life either for us to help them or them to help us and it always works both ways. Louise died five days before my 1st anniversary and I know that my higher power has placed her in my life to help me get sober and learn how AA works.

Not everyone in AA wants an Army sergeant for a sponsor. But the high percentages of AA members who have sponsors and who sponsor others, both in this sample and in AA in general, indicate that the sponsorship relationship—the close guidance of one individual's awakening to a new way of life by someone who has already gone through the process—is one of the most personal and powerful parts of the AA experience.

The appeal of the sponsorship relationship comes through, even when such a relationship has not been ideal. While some women have found sponsorship very meaningful, other women, almost with regret, mention that their experience with having a sponsor was not significant. One woman's comments serve almost as the inverse of the relationship with Louise described above. She wrote:

> At various times working my program, support of friends in AA has been helpful, but my relationship with sponsors has been less helpful than many people report theirs to be. I think there are many reasons for this: a result of moving from one city to another, as a result of my not being open, or probably also a result of poor choices. The sponsors either drink or just fade away. Sometimes I believe I go toward very needy women themselves and find the relationship too demanding for me in terms of their issues. However, I know many women who have extremely strong programs and I readily turn to them for guidance and support. While my own experience as a sponsor has not been dramatic, I found each experience quite rewarding.

Still other women have ambivalent relationships with their sponsors. One woman wrote:

> I did have a sponsor during that first year, someone who approached me rather than the other way around. I thought of her as a girlfriend. I really had no idea what I was doing, much less what a sponsor should do. There were women in the program who sponsored in a very hard-nosed, militant fashion and I didn't want any part of that. When I called someone up with a problem, I didn't want to be directed to literature or given orders. When I was experiencing a problem, first and foremost I wanted someone to listen, be a friend, a good, sober friend. My AA sponsor dropped me after I had my second slip. She also was miffed because I had gotten married without consulting her. I know now that she was trying, and doing her best, but these are complicated relationships. She later slipped herself, married a man in the program, and came to me to make an amends. I was a little puzzled about it at the time but I understand now that amends are important to the person making them. They don't have to make sense to the other person.

Another woman shared what her feelings and experience has been in sponsoring others:

For several years, when women approached me about sponsoring them, I would tell them that I couldn't be a traditional sponsor but that I can be a friend. It doesn't always work out. Early on, I had women in AA call on me whose problem with alcohol was secondary to other problems such as drugs, sexual orientation, and other addictions. I found that I could not help with these problems and had to ask them to find someone else to help. But in several cases, it has worked out. I have been actively sponsoring for about five years now and I find that I can be helpful and that it has helped me enormously. When two women are both working the AA program, they have a common language, experience, to draw on. It's very important for a person in recovery to be able to talk to someone who can totally relate to and understand their problems. I know people in the program who have several sponsors for different problems, AA, Al Anon, eating disorders, or other addictions.

The relationships that the women in this survey have developed with their sponsors, for good or for ill are a significant part of their sobriety. The percentage of women who sponsor other women and who have sponsors themselves is almost exactly the same as the figures for AA as a whole. They participate in the full range of Twelfth-Step activities and are even overrepresented in service positions, such as GSR, which traditionally require more time sober and are viewed as "more responsible" positions within AA's largely anti-hierarchical organizational system. There is nothing in the Twelfth-Step and sponsorship experiences of these women to indicate anything like second-class citizenship within AA and everything to indicate the full incorporation of women in an AA culture that they have helped to shape and sculpt to meet their particular needs.

The Role of Religion and Spirituality

AA calls itself a spiritual program of action. To members of AA, alcoholism is an illness which only a spiritual experience can conquer (Alcoholics Anonymous 1976, 44). Therefore, if an alcoholic works the Twelve Steps, she will have a spiritual awakening and will be able to maintain sobriety by continuing to identify personal defects of character, by working to enhance her awareness of the God of her understanding, and by helping other alcoholics and by practicing the principles of AA in all her affairs (the Tenth, Eleventh, and Twelfth Steps). To this end, the members of AA come to identify with some form of spirituality regardless of whether they identify with an organized religious belief. The survey materials for this research project included questions designed to gauge the relationship between religion and spirituality, as it is practiced and understood by the female members of AA. The survey material included standard questions and measures of religious and spiritual practice—such as religious affiliation, frequency of worship attendance, belief in God, feeling of closeness to God, and extent of prayer. Also, analysis of qualitative statements provided by the women will help to inform and explain how AA members utilize both religion and spirituality in their recovery from alcoholism.

In terms of religious affiliation, this sample of women is on par with the findings from General Social Survey (GSS) 1998 (see table 6.2). However, this sample has fewer Protestants and more women who reported "none" than those women surveyed in the GSS. Just over forty percent of this sample of women in AA identified themselves as Protestant, while over 57 percent of the women from the GSS called themselves Protestants. Also, more than 17 percent of this sample of women in AA reported their religious preference as "none" and 11 percent of the GSS sample reported "none." Both samples had similar numbers of self-identified Catholics. Both samples, too, have few women who identify themselves as Jewish or adherents of an Eastern religion. The remaining significant category includes those women who identified "other" as their religious preference. More women from the AA sample fell into this category than did the women from the GSS sample. These women in AA referred to no specific religion, but rather wrote that they believe in a mixture of religious or spiritual beliefs. For example, one woman remarked, "I dabble in Christianity, Judaism, and Eastern beliefs. Another woman wrote "I am a mix of many religions," and another woman characterized her beliefs as "potluck." Still other women in the AA sample do not identify a conventional religious denomination, but believe in spirituality. For example, one woman wrote that she has an "eclectic belief that all existence is spiritual and sacred." A couple of women remarked that they are either an ex-Catholic or a "lapsed Catholic," and a couple other women refer to being non-denominational or "just Christian." Another couple of women said that they belong to the Unitarian church, and one woman is a Quaker. While Christians predominate in both samples, the array of beliefs and the significant proportion with individualized belief systems in the AA sample of women, those who fall under either "None" or "Other" (30 percent of the total), indicates that there is room in AA for different definitions of God, religion, and spirituality.

When asked to characterize their feelings or beliefs about God, nearly two-thirds of the respondents indicated that the statement coming

Table 6.2 Comparison of religious affiliation between women in AA and the General Social Survey (percent)

Variable/Value	Women in AA	GSS
Religious Affiliation		
Protestant	40.6	57.8
Catholic	25.5	25.6
Jewish	3.6	1.6
Eastern	1.2	.5
None	17.6	11.0
Other	11.5	3.5
Total N	(167)	(1,217)

Source: General Social Survey 1998, women only.

closest to their beliefs was "I know God really exists and I have no doubts about it." Another 15 percent reported that "While I have doubts, I feel that I do believe in God." Taken together, these figures yield an overwhelming total of nearly eight in ten respondents in this survey who believe in God. Moreover, another 10 percent of the women report that, although they don't believe in a personal God, they do believe in a higher power of some kind (see table 6.3). Similarly, a small group among these women, just over 5 percent, provided a narrative statement of what they believe in, and all referred to spirituality in some sense. Also, 3 percent of the women sampled wrote that they find themselves believing in God some of the time, but not at other times. Two women selected the response "I don't know if there is a God and I don't believe there is a way to find out." But only one woman out of 167 reported that she does not believe in God. We know that AA presents itself as a spiritual program and that it contends that only a higher power can relieve the alcoholic of the obsession to drink. So, it is not so surprising that the women in this sample believe in God or a higher power and that very few doubt the existence of God or a higher power. Still, the high degree of certitude about the existence of God expressed by these women is extraordinary. Counting those whose belief system includes a higher power, but not a personal God, over 90 percent have few or no doubts about the existence of some kind of higher power. These data are consistent with the GSS, as American women in general appear to have little reservation about the belief in the existence of God or a higher power.

Indicative of their widespread and deep-rooted conviction about the existence of a higher spiritual source are the responses of those who previously indicated that they do not identify with a specific religion. Despite the absence of any organized religious belief system, they nonetheless report having a belief in God or a higher power. Fifteen of the twenty-nine women answered with "I know God really exists and I have no doubts about it." Another six selected "I don't believe in a personal God, but I do believe in a higher power of some kind."

When asked to pick the statement that "comes closest to expressing what you believe about God," four women of the twenty-nine who do not profess a specific religious faith gave their own narrative responses about their beliefs. One of the four women wrote "I believe in a higher power whom I choose to call God." Another woman wrote, "I can't pretend to 'know' what God is, therefore I can't believe in any one way or thing or explanation. . . I would go for a spiritual teaching that would include all as equals and to keep an open mind toward others in the world—acceptance and forgiveness." The third woman who is currently working on the Third Step wrote "I have no concept at this time. I am engaged in exploration of the issue." Finally, the fourth woman shared that, "I believe God isn't a person, but a positive energy, force, we tap into and benefit from . . . ." It is clear that, although these twenty-nine women do not identify themselves as belonging to a religion, they do nonetheless believe in God or a higher power. Therefore, almost every woman in the total sample of 167 holds either a specific religious or a generalized spiritual belief in God or a higher power.

Given that women in AA believe in God or a higher power, does having this belief in God or a higher power equate to women also feeling close to God? Apparently, yes, they not only have a strong belief in God or a higher power, but also feel very close or at least somewhat close to this entity (see table 6.4). Eight-seven women or over 52 percent report that they feel very close to God. Another fifty-nine women or just over 35 percent report feeling somewhat close to God. Over seven out of every eight women in this survey, then, indicate a sense of closeness and comfort with the God of their understanding. Since some 2 percent of the respondents did not answer the question as instructed, less than 10 percent of the survey respondents do not feel close to God, as they define God. Given that a significant proportion of the survey has not yet finished the steps (completing the first nine steps

Table 6.3 Comparison of the belief in God between women in AA & the General Social Survey (percent)

Variable/Value	Women in AA	GSS
I know God really exists and I have no doubts.	64.7	73.9
While I have doubts, I feel that I do believe in God.	15.0	13.1
I find myself believing in God some of the time, but not at other times.	3.0	2.8
I don't believe in a personal God, but I do believe in a higher power of some kind.	10.2	6.1
I don't know whether there is a God and I don't believe there is a way to find out.	1.2	2.4
I don't believe in God.	0.6	1.7
None of the above presents what I believe; What I believe about God is...	5.4	----
Total N	(167)	(654)

Source: General Social Survey, 2000, women only.

and then continuing to use the last three steps on a daily basis), these figures express an extraordinary degree of intimacy and comfort on the part of these women with their understanding of God.

Prayer and Meditation

There is no doubt about the habits of prayer and meditation among women in this sample. Just over 95 percent of the women surveyed pray one or more times a week. More specifically, over eight in ten pray or meditate every day and this far exceeds the daily practices of women surveyed in the GSS. In addition, close to one in ten pray two to three times per week, and another roughly 5 percent pray or meditate one time per week. In total, then, less than 5 percent of this survey group prays less frequently than once a week (see table 6.4). A minuscule 1 percent of the women pray less than once a year. This study did not ask them to indicate how they pray or meditate. However, some information about prayer is known. For example, each time an AA member attends an AA meeting, she has the opportunity to pray. The "Lord's Prayer" is said out loud, collectively by all members who choose to do so at the end of each meeting. Also, members of AA are encouraged to pray or meditate as part of their recovery program. The Third, Seventh, and Eleventh Steps include a prayer that is written into the discussion of the step in the text *Alcoholics Anonymous*. Although a member may or may not actually use these prayers either in completing a step or practicing a step on a daily basis, they are available for those who prefer to use a structured prayer. Also, the so-called Serenity Prayer is widely used among members of AA.

As far as the practices of prayer undertaken by women in AA are concerned, they are quite varied. The traditional Christian prayer practice of praying on one's knees is still mentioned in AA meetings, although the particular practices of prayer and meditation are not specifically defined. In fact, it is not until the Eleventh Step that the AA member is encouraged to continue to develop her spiritual program through prayer and meditation. For those who object to or are just not comfortable with prayer, meditation is an option. A publisher that is not endorsed by AA but which carries twelve-step related materials has published daily meditation books for women and other alcoholics. This type of literature is widely used by women to begin a program of meditation. Other tools or instructions on how to pray are found in the literature of AA, in the suggestions shared by members in the meetings, especially step meetings, and of course AA members may refer to their own church or spiritual advisor for information on how to pray and meditate.

Prayer is not a cure-all for women in AA. It is simply a tool to use in seeking emotional and spiritual well-being. The following excerpt was provided by a woman who continues to struggle with mental illness in addition to trying to maintain her sobriety. She gave her own perspective on the use of prayer in her life:

> The serenity prayer does not promise us happiness eternal, only that we might be reasonably happy in this life. My life has been better since I do not have to use alcohol on a daily basis and I feel I have alternatives to get through the slings and arrows of life without a drink. I feel that my life today is better without drinking even though I am facing not just the loss of a career path, but everything that it stood for—the promise of prestige, money, dignity, growth, etc. that goes along with the ability to follow a career path to its end. I see a door closing, perhaps a window will open.

In summary, with regards to religious affiliation, the largest proportion of women in this sample is Protestant, and the only other significant denomination in percentage terms is Catholic. Religious affiliation aside, when asked simply, "What do you feel about God," almost 80 percent of this sample said they believe in God and another 10 percent believe in a higher power. Also, over half of the women surveyed feel very close to God and another one-third of the sample feel somewhat close. Women in this sample, overwhelmingly not only have a strong belief in a personal God or a higher power, but they also feel that they have a close relationship with God or a higher power. Even more noteworthy is the fact that over 95 percent of the women in this sample pray or meditate one or more times a week.

Table 6.4 Comparison of other religious indicators between women in AA & the General Social Survey (percent)

Variable/Value	Women in AA	GSS
How close do you feel to God?		
Very close	52.1	43.1
Somewhat close	35.3	31.7
Not close	6.6	7.1
Does not believe	3.6	----
As close as possible	----	18.1
No answer	2.4	----
Total N	(167)	(706)
Frequency of Prayer and Meditation		
Everyday	81.4	55.7
Two to three times per week	9.0	13.6
One time per week	4.8	9.6
Twice a month to once quarterly	3.6	12.1
Less than once per year	1.2	9.0
Total N	(167)	(690)

Source: General Social Survey 1993 "Close to God" and 1998 "Frequency of Prayer." Note: The GSS offers more detailed categories under "Frequency of Prayer" than what is presented in this table.

Conclusion

These women in AA are very active in the service aspects of the twelve-step recovery program. They utilize the tools provided by AA to develop their own spiritual programs and 'pass on' to other women, what they too have been given—sobriety based on a spiritual orientation to the world. Although some innovations can be seen in how women work the last three steps of the program, these women seek to enhance their spirituality primarily through the same tools that AA members in general utilize. Lastly, the role of sponsorship is important to these women and it provides the opportunity for women to connect with each other and in some cases form an intimate relationship with other women. Although this special relationship is not particular only to women in AA, it does nevertheless display how one alcoholic woman can help another alcoholic woman to develop the power to overcome her addiction.

Notes

[1] Fifty-five women had not reached the Eleventh Step.

[2] After the first twenty-five questionnaires had been disseminated, the survey instrument was modified to include prayer on the list of spiritual activities connected with the Eleventh Step. As a result, the actual sample for this item is ninety-three.

[3] The specific spiritual program was not identified.

[4] AA is quided by Twelve Traditions and the Fifth Tradition reads, "Each group has but one primary purpose–to carry its message to the alcoholic who still suffers."

[5] Sixty-six women had not completed the Twelfth Step.

[6] The exact figures here are seventy-four women out of one hundred. The questionnaire was modified to include this item after eleven questionnaires had been received from women who had completed the Twelfth Step.

7

Conclusion: Empowering Women, Collectively and Individually

The experiences of the alcoholic women who participated in this survey provide a rich collection of material for considering twelve-step recovery a friend to feminism. The survey instrument used in this study and the data collected have supplied a thorough demographic description of the sample, providing both the context for this concluding analysis and a point of comparison with other studies. By means of both qualitative and quantitative methodologies, the past histories and the "lived" experiences of these women provide a further contextual and comparative base. Those materials help to explain how these women recovered from alcoholism despite the male-dominated environment of AA. In contrast to the interpretations of some feminist scholarship, these women exhibited very strong feminist beliefs and feminist behaviors. These two characteristics reveal themselves in action in the way that these women worked the Twelve Steps and in the forms and functions of the spirituality that they came to believe in and practice. The result is that these women have not succumbed, surrendered, or submitted to any form of belief or behavior that was not fully consistent with their own values, including feminist values. Rather, they have actually empowered themselves by working the Twelve Steps of AA. This same empowered approach characterized their participation in the larger twelve-step culture and in other modalities of recovery, a point of particular emphasis in feminist studies critical of women's involvement in AA and other twelve-step movements. This closing chapter will offer one final test upon which to gauge the nature of empowerment experienced by these women in AA from both a collective and an individual perspective. The first section will provide an analysis of feminism as measured by gender roles and other indices typically associated with second-wave feminist definitions of empowerment. The second section will discuss other personal forms of empowerment as described by this sample of women in AA. Finally, in light of the findings presented, a closing summary response to the second-wave feminist critique of the Twelve Steps and the wider twelve-step culture is presented.

Measures of Feminist Empowerment: Gender Roles

It is clear at this point in the research that this sample of women in recovery is very active in AA and does what is necessary to protect its sobriety. However, does this commitment to AA come at the cost of maintaining or developing other forms of collective empowerment— namely a feminist consciousness? One of the clearest ways that a feminist consciousness among women reveals itself is in their gender-role orientation. In addition to fighting for equal rights, equal pay, and equal opportunity, liberal feminists also battled against traditional gender roles for women and men, because these gender roles held women back from exercising equal opportunities. According to second-wave liberal feminists, women should not confine themselves exclusively to careers as housewives and mothers; they need to develop other roles for themselves, particularly work roles. Consequently, a benchmark of the success of the liberal feminist movement is the shift of women away from full-time domestic roles toward full-time occupational roles. Women's participation in the American labor force has grown over 20 percent since the 1950s and currently women make up nearly half of the work force (U.S. Department of Labor, March 2000). Debate still surrounds this expansion of women's roles, and the discussion is most heated when working mothers with young children are involved.

The findings from both this sample of women in AA and a sample of American women from the general public show the most ambiguity about gender roles, too, when small children are involved. However, without a doubt, this sample of women in AA holds strong feminist views on gender roles, including when women have young children at home. Measured utilizing four statements taken from the General Social Survey, over 92 percent of this sample of women from AA strongly disagreed or disagreed with putting the husband's career first. Eighty percent of this sample believes that a working mother can have just as close relationship with her child as a mother who does not work, and 82 percent strongly disagreed or disagreed with the statement that the man should be the achiever outside the home, while the woman takes care of the home and family. Although not as strong, a majority of over 60 percent of the women strongly disagreed or disagreed that a preschool child will suffer if the mother works. Overall, women in this sample of AA have a feminist gender-role orientation.

Table 7.1 Comparison of gender roles between women in AA & the General Social Survey (percent)

Variable/Values	Women in AA	GSS
Working mom may have warm relationship with child		
strongly agree	43.0	25.0
agree	40.5	41.0
disagree	14.0	27.0
strongly disagree	2.5	7.0
Total N	(167)	(1,058)
Husband's career first		
strongly agree	1.2	2.5
agree	6.1	16.9
disagree	34.1	51.2
strongly disagree	58.6	29.4
Total N	(167)	(1,031)
Best if man achieves outside the home, woman take care of home.		
strongly agree	2.5	11.0
agree	15.5	28.5
disagree	37.3	39.0
strongly disagree	44.7	21.5
Total N	(167)	(1,031)
Preschool child suffers if mother works		
strongly agree	4.4	8.2
agree	34.8	33.4
disagree	39.3	45.0
strongly disagree	21.5	13.4
Total N	(167)	(1,037)

Source: General Social Survey (GSS), 2000 edition, women only.
Note: Data for "Husband's career first" comes from the 1998 edition.

Measures of Feminist Empowerment: Other Indices

In addition to measuring attitudes toward gender roles, this study asked four more questions to help evaluate whether women in AA have a feminist consciousness. The first question involves the issue of self-identification, asking whether women consider themselves feminists. Question two deals with matters that are more practical, but still involve aspects of self-identification, inquiring whether the feminist movement has improved their lives. The third and fourth questions relate more to active involvement in feminist concerns, asking how much they pay attention to news items related to women's issues and how much they participate in activities related specifically to women's issues. Taken together, these questions serve as an index of feminist consciousness held by women in AA.

Feminist Identity

Given the high commitment to feminist positions discussed in the preceding section on attitudes concerning gender roles, it would be consistent to expect high levels of self-identification as feminists from the women in this survey. That expectation would be misplaced, however, because these women shy away from a feminist identification. In response to the question, "Do you consider yourself a feminist?" just over one-half of the AA sample answered affirmatively. This closely divided statistic is not consistent with the previous findings in this study. Therefore, further analysis is needed in order to decipher the underlying meaning of these seemingly incongruous responses to gender-role issues and to feminism.

In the open-ended section of this question, the majority of women who think of themselves as feminists referred to their belief in equal opportunities between the sexes. Half of those women, twenty-six out of fifty-two, used the terms equal, equality, equal rights, or equal opportunities in their statements. Some statements provided by these respondents referred to equality in domestic roles. Equality of ability and the right to equality of opportunity and treatment are central to the world views of the women in this survey who identified themselves as feminists.

A few women answered with interpretations of their own experience. For example, one woman writes with pride of her achievements and her role as a trend setter:

With a doctorate in chemistry I worked for over 30 years before I retired from federal service. I was a pioneer (I think of myself as one.) In the 1960's and the 1970's I was the only woman among my peers most of the time. My daughter had babysitters and went to nursery school, very unusual for those times.

Many of those women who reject the feminist label do so, because they deny having a specifically gendered consciousness. These women either believe in equality for all without regard to gender or consider themselves humanists without needing to enter gender into the equation. The statement that follows may be characterized as "Golden Rule humanism":

I am not pro woman or man—I'm pro God and me—and do the best I can to contribute to life for me and others in a positive way and I believe I am a person to be treated as I would treat anyone else who isn't hurtful, or harmful to others. I favor respect, empathy, kindness, and good manners.

The second most frequent response of those who reject the feminist label came from ten women who affirmed traditional gender and family roles. However, several of these women, while expressing their belief in more traditional gender and family roles, stated that they also believed in equality in the work place. For example:

I believe in traditional roles in the area of home and family, but not the workplace. I enjoy being a woman. I enjoy chivalry and traditional romance and (one day) motherhood. However, I will always have a job for my own self worth to stay in tact.

Another group of women who do not consider themselves feminists state that they do not consider themselves active enough to be feminists, question the value of identification with the movement, or question the label of feminist. Five women reflect an expectation that to be feminist is to be politically active. Even those women who call themselves "feminists" questioned the meaning of the term. For example one woman writes, "I am not sure what a feminist is." Another woman qualifies her "yes" response by stating, "I am not a radical or militant, but yes, a feminist." Similarly, another respondent writes "Yes, but not in the hard core sense, I feel I have inherited and take for granted (in the sense that these choices were granted me always) the initial feminist movement beginning in the 60's." There is a certain sense of unease

**Table 7.2 Comparison of feminist indicators between women in AA &
the General Social Survey (percent)**

Variable/Value	Women in AA	GSS
Do you consider yourself a feminist?		
Yes	52.2	28.7
No	47.7	71.3
Feminist movement improved your life?		
Improved	94.4	47.2
Made worse	----	4.0
No impact	5.6	48.7
Do you pay attention to women's issues in the news?		
Very Often	47.9	28.0
Fairly Often	35.8	41.0
Sometimes	2.1	----
Not Too Often	4.2	27.0
Never	0	4.0
Total N	(167)	(792)

*Notes: GSS data are from the 1996 survey, which are the most
recent for this question. Response categories for the AA sample
under "Feminist movement improved life" included three separate
conditions—a lot, somewhat, and a little—and have been collapsed
into simply "improved" for comparison purposes.*

about embracing the feminist label that pervades these answers. Overall,
this group of women, whether they accept of reject the feminist label,
qualify their responses based on their perception that to be feminist is to
be a political activist and that this political association is tied to the
second-wave of the feminist movement.

Although this sample of women does not appear to be remarkably
ideological, they do not seem to be apolitical, apathetic or otherwise

disengaged from issues of concern to the feminist movement, either. Elaine Rapping (1996) and others have charged that women in the twelve-step programs are subject to a patriarchal culture which projects traditional views onto women. The results of this survey clearly suggest that only a small group of women in this sample believe in traditional gender and family roles. Moreover, four of the ten women who provided a written response supporting traditional family roles also believed in working outside the home for their own independence. Additionally, while almost one-half of the alcoholic women in AA surveyed for this study do not consider themselves feminists, the General Social Survey (1996) of the U.S. population revealed that almost three out of four American women reject the designation feminist (see table 7.2). Therefore, in spite of any potentially anti-feminist effects of the recovery environment, these women in AA have a much stronger identification with being feminist than women in the general U.S. population.

Life Improved & Feminist News

Another way of gauging the feminist inclinations of the women in this survey was to ask them to assess the impact that the feminist movement has had on their lives. The question asked specifically, "To what extent do you feel the feminist movement has improved your life?" An astonishing 95 percent of the women in this survey think that the feminist movement has improved their lives.

A third indicator of feminist consciousness is the extent to which women pay attention to women's issues. The women in this sample were asked, "When reading, watching, or listening to the news, how often do you pay attention to issues that especially affect women?" Almost 95 percent of these women turn their attention to news stories about issues that affect women with a frequency ranging from sometimes to very often. These figures indicate a substantial interest in such matters. Once again, when compared to the figures for the GSS sample from 1996, the women in this survey showed higher levels of behaviors that can be identified as feminist (see table 7.2). Judging by the extent of their attention to women's issues in the news, it appears that the women in this sample care about women's issues in numbers much higher than the percentage who identify themselves as feminists. In spite of what they call themselves (feminist or non-feminist), the behavior of these women demonstrates that they possess feminist values and orientations.

Feminist Activities

The final indicator of feminist consciousness used in this study measures the extent that women in AA participate in activities related to women's issues. The question used to gauge this participation asked the women "What kinds of activities have you engaged in, while in sobriety, which are related to women's issues?" Over 70 percent of the women who were surveyed for this study had engaged in at least one such activity in sobriety. These activities are diverse, ranging from donations to organizations that serve women to attending a public rally or meeting relating to women's rights (see table 7.3). Whatever the activity— whether it be a joining a club or business group, attending an educational event or a community association meeting, or writing a public official—all of these activities reflect a level of involvement with both women's issues and with the on-going pursuit of women's rights.

Table 7.3 Summary of the top five feminist activities engaged in by women in AA (percent)

Variable/Value	Women in AA
What kinds of activities have you engaged in, while in sobriety related to women's issues?	
Give money to an organization serving women	37.7
Gather informally with other women to talk about concerns of women	37.7
Join clubs or activities that are attended primarily by women	28.1
Attend educational events to learn more about women's issues	22.8
Attend a public rally, demonstration, or women's rights meeting	22.2
Total N	(117)

Note: Responses were not limited to one answer only. Just over seventy percent of these women in AA have participated in at least one activity.

Far more than merely identifying with the term feminist or even following stories related to women in the news, activities such as these indicate an awareness of and concern about issues that affect them because of their gender.

A substantial portion of feminist literature on AA and other twelve-step programs contends that the culture of these programs is traditional, male-dominated, and personal. As a result, the literature concludes, the growth and development of the culture of recovery is inimical to the continued vitality and strength of feminism. The purpose of this final test has been to discuss feminist attitudes, behaviors, and self-identification among this study's sample of women in AA. If, as the feminist literature critical of AA would have it, the culture of AA is such that it promotes traditional gender roles and anti-feminist sentiment, then it would be expected that any sample of women in AA would be weak in feminist consciousness. This is not so. Moreover, women in this sample were not just on par with the GSS sample, but were substantially more feminist on measures of gender roles, feminist identification, and attention given to women's issues. Additionally, women in this sample are very engaged in activities related to women's issues. All of this evidence suggests that involvement in AA and the larger twelve-step movement has not driven a wedge between these women and feminist ideals once advocated by second-wave liberal feminists.

Forms of Personal Empowerment

In addition to a collective, or second-wave, conception of empowerment, this research sought to include a more personal or individual account of empowerment as experienced by women in AA. This qualitative analysis will extend the construct of empowerment to include the many different ways in which women experience personal growth in AA. In addition to regaining a sense of self-esteem, the women who participated in this survey benefited in a variety of ways from getting sober in AA. They were asked, "After not drinking, what are some of the good things that have resulted from your sobriety?" In their responses, they indicated an array of good things that came into their lives, after the destruction and chaos of alcoholic drinking was exchanged for the fellowship and program of AA (see table 7.6). These good things ranged from improved relationships to general enjoyment of life and gratitude. In the following section, the good things that these women have received are presented. The bulk of this section consists of the women expressing in their own voices how their lives have changed for the better. First of all, the women state in their own words that their self-esteem has improved as a result of their sobriety. Next, the women in this sample tell about their improved relationships with men and with family members. Thirdly, the women identify that their jobs and careers have developed as a result of recovery. Fourth, these women speak about spirituality and how they have developed it in their lives. Next, physical and mental health is attributed to sobriety. Finally, enjoyment and gratitude toward AA and life is celebrated by these women.

Table 7.4 Summary of other good things experienced by women in AA (percent)

Variable/Value	Women in AA
After not drinking, what are some of the good things that have resulted from sobriety?	
Better relationships	49.3
Improved job or career	30.8
Developed spiritual life	22.6
Improved physical health	15.3
Mental health recovery	14.0
General positive outlook on life	11.3
Serenity and peace of mind	7.3
Total N	(151)

Note: Responses were not limited to one answer only.

Self-Esteem

Empowerment of women in AA can be seen most easily in their personal statements about improved self-esteem and self-respect as a result of their sobriety and membership in AA. Almost a quarter of the respondents stated that their self-esteem, self-respect, self worth, or confidence in themselves had improved.[1] Sixteen women specifically used the word self-esteem. Some women gave behavioral examples of their improved sense of self. For example, one woman wrote, "I am more self-confident. I just went off to Africa for eight weeks to give a training course." A second woman stated, "I have more self-esteem, self-respect, responsibility, returned to school for a higher degree, and traveled." A third woman wrote, "I have positive self-esteem, outlook, choices, dreams and vision to become totally self-sufficient, and I a full time entrepreneur serving seniors/women and children at risk."

Other women expressed that they still have to fight to feel good about themselves, but that they have made progress. One woman shared, "I have more self-esteem and I am more forgiving of my shortcomings. I try not to beat myself up so much." Another woman admitted "Even though I still have a self-defeating attitude, it is now balanced with recognition of my good qualities. I've gotten a degree..." Another woman described how far she had come in terms of self-esteem. She referred to the self-esteem scale on the questionnaire and wrote "answers to self-esteem are at a greater level than I would have placed them when I first came to AA. I rated myself somewhere lower than whale shit." Lastly, two women commented on how self-esteem affected the view and relationship one has with one's self. The first woman remarked, "I have much better self-esteem and I am no longer ashamed of myself as a whole person. The second woman simply offered, "My relationship with myself is healthier." Overall, these women have regained or are regaining self-esteem, self-respect, self worth, self-confidence, and a sense of self. These processes are essential to the development of personal empowerment and a sense of one's self as a full and whole person.

Improved Relationships

Leading the column of good things that sobriety has brought was improved relationships. In fact, virtually half of the responses in this sample included statements that these women had better relationships with family and friends. Over one-fifth of the respondents specified having better relationships with their children. One woman stated, "I have renewed relationships with my children," while another woman exclaimed, "I have a wonderful relationship with my children." In one instance the woman remarked, "I have a relationship with my son after deserting him to my parents." Another woman reported, "My children want to spend time with me." Several women mentioned improved relationships with their boyfriends or husbands. One of them replied "Saved my marriage." Another woman noted, "I have a healthy relationship with a new husband." With hope for the future, one woman exclaimed "I was able to love a man who I would never have been open to before sobriety. We are now married and hope to start a family." After significant bad experiences in the past, another woman was able to report that, "After two failed marriages of 3 years each, I have a 20 year marriage in sobriety." A couple more women told of having closer relationships with other women. For example, one woman wrote, "I have close friendships with other women, in and out of recovery." Another woman simply stated, "I have relationships with women." No matter whom the relationship is with, as one woman stated, "I have strong positive and supportive relationships with men and women." Lastly, one woman summarized "My relationships are of a higher quality."

Over all, relationships are very important to women in recovery. Many women damaged their relationships with family members, including husbands, children, parents, and grandparents. Recovery has afforded them the opportunity of making amends and of correcting any past wrongs (Ninth Step). Moreover, as women develop more self-esteem and confidence, they also get better at recognizing and acknowledging what is a good and healthy relationship and what is not.

Improved Spirituality

In reference to the development of spirituality, between a fifth and a quarter of the women responded that it is a good thing to have developed their spiritual life. For some women this means having a belief or faith in God or a higher power. For example, one woman merely wrote "I have a faith in God," while another woman explained more fully that "I have a belief in the sustained power of faith." Two women simply expressed "I have a relationship with my higher power." For other women, it is a good thing to have a general sense of spirituality in their lives. For example, three women reflected in very similar terms that, "I have a strong spiritual foundation" and "I have a spiritual basis for my life," and finally, "I have a spiritual life for which I am comfortable." For other women, spirituality is having meaning in their lives or, as one woman wrote, "A sense of being."

In addition to the thirty-four women who view spiritual development as a good thing, eleven other women noted that they have serenity and peace of mind as a result of sobriety and AA. Generally, women mentioned having serenity in relation to having a spiritual awareness and having an acceptance of oneself. For example, one woman wrote "serenity and peace with who I am and others are." A second woman wrote "I have a real sense of belonging, happiness, serenity." A third woman stated "I have self worth, serenity, open mindedness, socially welcomed, closer to God, acceptance of self and others, peaceful co-existence." Not all women have attained absolute serenity, but they keep working for it. Three different women expressed this same idea in different ways. One wrote, "some piece of mind, some serenity," a second noted that she has "moments of serenity," while the third reported that she has "occasionally true serenity." Serenity is discussed in relation to the Third Step and especially the Ninth Step in AA, and the so-called Serenity Prayer is often used in groups as an addition to the Lord's Prayer that is said out loud and collectively at the end of many meetings. Individuals also use the Serenity Prayer frequently. The concept of serenity as understood in AA can be summarized in the words of one of the respondents, who described her "inner peace."

These individual accounts of improvement in substantial areas of one's life can be deemed empowering by any measure. Certainly, second-wave feminist would agree that increased self-esteem, healthy relationships, and spiritual growth are worthy accomplishments that could arguably lead to personal empowerment. The means of this empowerment—the twelve-step program—deserves to be recognized as a potentially liberating process, even if not a political process. Individual empowerment occurs for each of these women in a very personal way and yet develops partially in response to their collective involvement in AA. Moreover, each of these women point to the Twelve Steps of AA as the foundation for their new-found sobriety and enjoyment of life.

A Final Note on Twelve-Step Work, Spirituality, and Feminism

It is now clear that in addition to liberal-feminist beliefs and actions, the women in this sample also experience a more personal type of empowerment as members of AA. It does not appear that holding feminist attitudes distracts from active participation in the twelve-step program of AA. Moreover, there is no evidence to support the claim that a spiritual program will divert women from collective or public action in other areas of their lives including issues of concern to women. However, it is also very clear, based on personal accounts, that these women value and deem empowering the development of a spiritual program based on the Twelve Steps of AA.

Rather than speaking of traditional religious beliefs or organized religions, the women in this sample refer to an open-ended development of faith and spirituality based on the Twelve Steps of AA. The flexibility in interpretation and practice of the Twelve Steps can be seen in how women proceed through the Twelve Steps of AA. Overall, women in this sample did not succumb easily to the process of developing a spiritual program based on the Twelve Steps. Women in AA struggled with the ideas represented in the Twelve Steps, as they worked through them. For example, most of the women had difficulty with the First

Step, because they would not or could not recognize their powerlessness over alcohol until after they had relapsed, hit bottom, or otherwise finally broken through the psychological denial of their disease. The most cited explanation for the women's difficulty was their inability to let go of the illusion that they could control their drinking. As was true of the First Step, most of the women who had completed the Third Step thought it difficult. The reasons for this difficulty centered on the resistance to turning "our will and our lives over to God." Despite the broad tolerance encompassed in the phrase "as we understood Him," these women had problems trusting in a higher power because of their pre-existing conceptions of what a higher power is, past experiences with authority figures, or simply because they lacked knowledge about the spiritual. Most importantly, women reported having to work this step on a daily basis, because it is difficult to turn their will over and not "take it back." This implies that the women in AA continue to use their own will power and that there remains a tension between theory and practice in surrendering one's life over to the care of God. The Fourth Step, too, was difficult for most of the women who had completed this step. Women did not want to look at themselves honestly and were afraid of what they would find in taking a moral inventory of themselves. Some of the women specifically spoke about shame and guilt feelings, which made this step particularly difficult. Almost three-quarters of the women who had completed this step adapted the step by including a list of character assets in addition to making a list of character defects. In spite of this, the Fourth Step was still difficult for women in this sample. The experiences of these women, with the first four steps, demonstrate that they did not submit themselves mindlessly and without reservation to these spiritual processes.

The experiences of these women with three other controversial steps—Eight, Eleven, and Twelve—reveal the same processes of resistance and flexible adaptation. Unlike the first four steps, the Eighth Step did not prove difficult for the women in this sample. According to their responses, by the time the women in this sample got to this step, they either already knew who they needed to make amends to or they did not have many amends to make, because they lived in isolation or kept their drinking primarily to themselves. Also, some of the women (a quarter) who had completed this step had included a list of those who had harmed them, in addition to those they had harmed. Similarly, the women also reported putting themselves on their list of amends to make, so that they could forgive themselves for their behavior prior to recovery. As regards the Eleventh and Twelfth Steps, these women report regular attendance at meetings, prayer, and reading AA literature as the three most practiced Eleventh-Step activities, and their three most common Twelfth-Step activities are responsibilities related to holding meetings, holding a group position, and sponsoring other women. In terms of their belief systems, most of the women believe in God, over half feel very close to God, and over one-third feel somewhat close to God. In general, these women have worked the Twelve Steps, have developed a belief in a higher power or God, and continue to develop their spiritual programs. But they do so not without resistance or without the exercise of their own will power. In sum, this sample of women in AA feels comfortable with both the culture and the spiritual practices of AA. They have adapted the steps to accommodate themselves, and have been fully engaged in both AA as a whole and the larger recovery movement.

Toward a Conclusion: The Larger Twelve-Step Culture and Feminism

Although the women in this sample were not specifically asked about their views about the larger twelve-step recovery movement, it is clear that these women in AA develop an orientation toward recovery from alcoholism that is much more comprehensive than just seeking abstinence from alcohol. For example, these women have utilized more than one twelve-step program, have sought help outside of AA, and have sought ways to develop healthy relationships with others. Also, the women in this sample report that they learn a lot about recovery by attending women-only meetings and listening to the experiences of other women in AA. Additionally, women in this sample believe that they express themselves more openly and freely than do the men in AA. This combination of willingness to seek recovery outside of AA, concern about developing their relationships with others, and an expressive communication style helps to explain why women become both consumers and producers of the twelve-step recovery movement.

Findings in this study suggest that women influence AA by bringing into AA meetings ideas, concepts, and language that is used in other twelve-step programs. For example, women seeking help outside of AA bring back into the meetings psychological concepts learned from the treatment community. Similarly, women who have participated in an addiction treatment program are introduced to both a clinical treatment language and to the twelve-step recovery language. Moreover, while in treatment, women are routinely exposed to non-AA literature and treatment exercises that integrate both the medical and the self-help approaches to recovery from alcoholism and other addictions. Therefore, learning about recovery does not happen only as a result of listening and articulating one's story in AA meetings, but knowledge about recovery is also developed through participation in professional treatment programs, reading recovery-oriented literature and completing exercises related to recovery. The expansion of the twelve-step movement has occurred, then, in an environment that is conducive to the integration of different mediums of learning and self-awareness, and women have been the most significant group shaping and transmitting these elements of different recovery cultures to new arenas.

Aside from exposure to the professional treatment community, women also attend other twelve-step programs that focus on relationships, such as Al-Anon, ACA, and CoDA. Involvement in these programs has greatly influenced the language and manner in which women discuss their personal empowerment in AA. Learning how to relate to self and others appears to be the most important aspect of recovery for many of the women surveyed. For the majority of women in AA, the issue is mostly about how to say "no" to others and how to resist putting other people's needs before one's own needs. Some of these women have to learn that they do not have to "fix" other people's problems, they do not have to "enable" another's individual abuse of alcohol or drugs, and they are entitled to just say "no" to the requests and needs of others. Nonetheless, simply stated, it remains difficult for women in recovery to change their people-pleasing orientation toward others and to put themselves first. Some women in AA express poorly defined ego boundaries by "acting out" sexually or in other self-destructive ways. These women tend to be younger, cross-addicted to other drugs and generally caught up in a self-destructive life style. Some of these women have experienced severe forms of childhood sexual abuse, and this "pattern" is continued into adulthood. However, once in recovery, these women are able to define balanced ego boundaries and become aware of what is healthy and not healthy for them. For all of these women building self-esteem and learning what is emotionally healthy leads to personal empowerment. This is the language of personal empowerment that has evolved over time within the twelve-step movement. It is also reflected in the written expressions provided by the women for this research project.

The findings in this study do not support the criticism that AA and the twelve-step community influence women negatively in terms of feminist empowerment. The experiences of the women who participated in this survey demonstrate that the criticisms of AA and the general twelve-step movement made by Rapping (1996) and some other feminist researchers that the twelve-step culture invites self-absorption and anti-feminist attitudes among its female members are not supported. Although the women in this sample work hard on both their emotional and spiritual recovery, they also score high in feminist beliefs and act in ways consistent with a feminist consciousness. Moreover, there is no data from this sample of women that supports the idea that women's participation in other twelve-step programs is corrosive to their feminist attitudes and behaviors. In addition, these women, while active in other twelve-step programs, are selective in the programs they attend and continue to attend AA much more frequently than any other program. These women are augmenting their recovery with other venues, but they do not seem to be "stuck" in the culture of recovery.

Norman Denzin maintains in *The Alcoholic Society: Addiction and Recovery of the Self* (1993) that two other twelve-step movements, ACA and CoDA, have had both a positive and a negative influence on women. He agrees with some critics who argue that some women get stuck in the twelve-step recovery ideology and continue to adopt negative definitions of themselves, such as being "codependent." His characterization of the effect of codependency captures the general feminist criticism against AA and the other twelve-step movements. He asserts that:

> Codependency fosters a new negative identity for women, asking them to assume a new form of illness with ambiguous psychological and behavioral dimensions. This process of medicalization then contributes to an ideology that recommends a lifelong process of recovery. For many women this is a no-exit model; they may remain trapped inside Al-Anon, CoDA or other recovery groups (1993, xii).

As has been seen, the women in this survey are more productive in their approach toward recovery than that characterization would imply. Their responses to the survey, data and their narratives, portray a process of recovery that may in fact be never-ending, but that brings with it finite, objective rewards and positive consequences that do not hinder their feminist consciousness and that do enhance their self-esteem. Denzin (1993) attributes the positive possibilities in the twelve-step movements directly to feminism and to the fact that:

> Women can now seek recovery identities outside of the family rather than be stuck in gender family roles of the 1950s and 1960s. . . . This is what the ideology of co-dependency and recovery gives them. In this movement lie kernels of radical social change. . . . Thus the terms and slogans of recovery from alcoholism (denial, discovery, codependency, no pain, no gain, good coming from bad) transcend the

specifics of alcoholism. They refer back to something deeper, namely the gendered selves and intimate relationships between men and women that this culture promotes (1993, xiii).

The women in this survey are deeply involved in a process of redefinition that places them in a new relationship to the world, including their relationships with the God of their personal understanding, with other women especially in AA, and, as their narratives so eloquently express, with their mates and their families. This is nothing less than Denzin's "progressive commitment to a transcendent perspective that constantly seeks new forms of self development" (1993, xiii).

It is the conclusion of this researcher that the women in AA successfully develop a recovery identity that liberates them in the positive way that Denzin describes. Moreover, the women in this sample not only seek a recovery identity, but they also undergo a life-changing experience that is very much like what women experience when they adopt a feminist identity. Bartky (1990, 11) states:

> To be a feminist, one has to become a feminist. For many feminists, this involves the experience of a profound personal transformation, an experience which goes far beyond that sphere of human activity we regard ordinarily as "political." This transforming experience, which cuts across ideological divisions within the women's movement, is complex and multi-faceted. In the course of undergoing the transformation to which I refer, the feminist changes her behavior: she makes new friends; she responds differently to people and events; her habits of consumption change; sometimes she alters her living arrangements or, more dramatically, her whole style of life.

If one were to substitute recovering alcoholic for feminist and twelve-step movement for the feminist movement, this passage would fit the recovering woman alcoholic perfectly. And the women in this sample have done just about everything that Bartky lists. As the individual stories of recovery and the survey data reveal, women in AA change their behavior as a result of working the Twelve Steps. They move from being self-destructive to self-protective. At first, they do this by simply not drinking one day at a time. In order to do this, they may in some instances change their friends. Initially, women stop associating with those who drink alcoholically, and, as they progress in sobriety, they begin to stop associating with those who hurt them either emotionally or otherwise. Over time in recovery, the woman learns how to respond differently to people and events in her life. Initially, she stays away from slippery places and situations that bring on anxiety, fear, or any other negative emotions from which she might want to escape by drinking. As she grows, the woman begins to set boundaries and defend herself in interpersonal relationships. In some instances, this results in changing living arrangements. Many of the women in this sample have gone through divorces in recovery, and many more have altered their relationships with men. Women in AA definitely change their consumption patterns: they learn not to use alcohol and other substances in addictive ways and begin to learn how to nurture themselves as women in constructive rather than self-destructive ways. This may include working other twelve-step programs in order to learn that sex, food, relationships, shopping, and many other "distractions" can all be forms of addictive behavior. Finally, women in AA develop what can be described as a form of feminist consciousness through the exchange of their experience, strength, and hope with each other. Through this exchange, women recognize among themselves what is healthy and self-protective behavior and what is not. In this way, women learn to assert themselves in their lives, and ultimately the act of emotional self-reliance is both an act of recovery and a feminist act.

In the final analysis, this sample of women in AA, in spite of their severe problems, earnestly work toward bettering themselves physically, emotionally and spiritually. The women are thirsty for personal growth, and at times this may lead them into areas of self-help consumption that prove to be excessive or not beneficial. For the most part, however, the women in this sample do not attend multiple twelve-step programs or even appear to be overly dependent on AA. In fact, it appears that, while attendance at AA meetings remains strong, women in AA develop very full, useful, and prosperous lives. Women who were once shameful alcoholics are now role models within their communities. Their backgrounds are varied, but their recoveries are similar. Almost all develop a connection with or a belief in God, a higher power, or some other power outside of themselves. Paradoxically, as they develop a trust in something outside of themselves, they develop the courage and strength first to stay sober and secondly to grow in all areas of their lives. Personal empowerment can be seen in every woman in this survey. Some women are still struggling to fight off the compulsion to drink or use a drug, but even they sense the relief of hope that they too will come to know a "new freedom and a new happiness" (Alcoholics Anonymous 1976, 83). Other women with more than twenty years of sobriety continue to come back to women's AA meetings and to share their experience, strength, and hope. This sharing between the new and the old in AA facilitates the personal transformation that women experience as members of AA that results from working the Twelve Steps. It is through this process that women in AA develop a stronger sense of self that is passed on from generation to generation of alcoholics in AA and that demonstrates that both collective and individual empowerment is beyond a doubt a primary outcome of participation in the twelve-step program of AA.

Notes

[1] There were 150 women who provided narrative responses to this portion of the survey.

Bibliography

Alcoholics Anonymous. 1952. *Twelve Steps and Twelve Traditions.* New York: Alcoholics Anonymous World Services, Inc.

____1962. *The A.A. service manual.* New York: Alcoholics Anonymous World Services, Inc.

____1976. *Alcoholics Anonymous.* 3rd edition. New York: Alcoholics Anonymous World Services, Inc.

2004. *Alcoholics Anonymous membership survey.* New York: Alcoholics Anonymous World Services, Inc.

American Society of Addiction Medicine (ASAM PPC-2R). 2000. *Patient Placement criteria for the treatment of substance-related disorders.* Chevy, Chase, MD

American Psychiatric Association. 1994. *Diagnostic and statistical manual of mental disorders, fourth edition.* Washington, DC: The Association.

Bartky, Sandra Lee. 1990. *Femininity and domination: studies in the phenomenology of oppression.* New York: Routledge.

Beattie, M. 1987. *Co-dependent no more.* New York: Harper & Row.

____1990. *Co-dependent's guide to the twelve steps.* New Jersey: Prentice Hall.

Bebko, Claudia. 1991. Introduction. In *Feminism and addiction.* New York: Hawthorn Press.

Bebko, Claudia and Jo-Ann Krestan. 1991. Codependency: the social reconstruction of female experience. In *Feminism and addiction.* ed. C. Bebko. New York: Hawthorn Press.

Beckman, Linda J. 1994. Treatment needs of women with alcohol problems. *Alcohol, Health and Research World.* 18 (3): 206-219.

Beckman, L. J., and K. M. Kocel. 1982. Treatment-delivery system and alcohol abuse in women: social policy implications. *Journal of Social Issues.* 38 (2): 139-151.

Belenky, Mary F., Blyth M. Clinchy, Nancy R. Goldberger, and Jill M. Tarule. 1986. *Women's way of knowing: the development of self, voice, and mind.* New York: Basic Books.

Berenson, David. 1991. Powerlessness—liberating or enslaving? Responding to the feminist critique of the Twelve Steps. In *Feminism and addiction.* C. Bebko, ed. 67-86. New York: The Hawthorn Press.

Blume, S. B. 1997. Women and alcohol: Issues in social policy. In *Gender and alcohol.* S. Wilsnack and R. Wilsnack, eds. 462-477. New Brunswick, NJ: Rutgers Center of Alcohol Studies.

Bryer, J. B., B. A. Nelson, J. B. Miller, and P. A. Krol. 1987. Childhood sexual and physical abuse as factors in adult psychiatric illness. *American Journal of Psychiatry.* 144: 1426-1430.

Bucholz, Kathleen K. 1992. Alcohol abuse and dependence from a psychiatric epidemiologic perspective. *Alcohol Health and Research World.* 16 (3): 197-208.

Catenao, R. 1994. Drinking and alcohol-related problems among minority women. *Alcohol, Health and Research World.* 18 (3): 233-241.

Copeland, J. and W. Hall. 1992. A comparison of predictors of treatment drop-out in a specialist women's and two traditional mixed-sex treatment services. *British Journal of Addictions.* 87: 883-890.

Covington, S. 1982. Sexual experience, dysfunction, and abuse: a comparative study of alcoholic and nonalcoholic women. Ph.D. dissertation, Department of Sociology, Union Graduate School.

Davis, Diane R. 1997. Women healing from alcoholism: a qualitative study. *Contemporary Drug Problems.* 24: 147-177.

Davis, James A. and T. Smith 2007. *General social surveys,* 1972-2006 [machine-readable data file] /Principal Investigator, James A. Davis; Director and Co-Principal Investigator, Tom W. Smith; Co-Principal Investigator, Peter V. Marsden; Sponsored by National Science Foundation. --NORC ed.-- Chicago: National Opinion Research Center [producer]; Storrs, CT: The Roper Center for Public Opinion Research, University of Connecticut [distributor].

Deming, M. P, N. D. Chase, and D. Karesh. 1996. Parental alcoholism and perceived levels of family health among college freshmen. *Alcoholism Treatment Quarterly.* 14: 47-57.

Denzin, N. K. 1987. *The recovering alcoholic.* Newbury Park, CA: Sage Publications.

_____1993. *The alcoholic society: addiction and recovery of the self.* New Brunswick, N.J.: Transaction Publishers.

Fagan, J. 1993. Interactions among drugs, alcohol, and violence. *Health Affairs.* 12: 65-79.

Faludi, Susan. 1991. *Backlash: the undeclared war against American women.* New York: Anchor Books.

Fox, K. M., and Gilbert, B. 0. 1994. The interpersonal and psychological functioning of women who experienced childhood physical abuse, incest, and parental alcoholism. *Child Abuse and Neglect.* 18: 849-858.

Fromberg, D., D. Gjerdingen, and M. Preston. 1986. Multiple roles and women's health: what have we learned? *Women and Health.* 11 (2): 79-96.

Garbarino, C., and C. Strange. 1993. College adjustment and family environments of students reporting parental alcohol problems. *Journal of College Student Development.* 34: 261-266.

Grant, B., H. Bergman, S. W. Glenn, A. L. Errico, and A. C. King. 1994. Prevalence of DSM-IV alcohol abuse and dependence. *Alcohol Health and Research World.* 18: 243-245.

Hall, C. W., L. M. Bolen, and R. E. Webster. 1994. Adjustment issues with adult children of alcoholics. *Journal of Clinical Psychology.* 50: 786-792.

Hallberg, Lillian M.. 1988. Rhetorical dimensions of institutional language: a case study of women alcoholics. Ph.D. dissertation, The University of Iowa.

Hanna, E. Z. 1991. Social opportunity and alcohol abuse in women: temporal and structural differences in drinking contexts of non clinic and clinic female drinkers. *Journal of Substance Abuse.* 3: 1-11.

Harford T., E. Hanna, and V. Faden. 1994. The long- and short-term effect of marriage on drinking. *Journal of Substance Abuse.* 6: 209-217.

Hezler, J. E., A. Burnham, and L. T. McEvoy. 1991. Alcohol abuse and dependence. In *Psychiatric disorders in America: the epidemiological catchment area study*. L. N. Robins and D. A. Regier, eds. 81-115. New York: The Free Press.

Hill, S.Y. 1984. Vulnerability to the biomedical consequences of alcoholism and alcohol-related problems among women. In: *Alcohol problems in women. Antecedents, consequences, and intervention*. S. C. Wilsnack and L. J. Beckman, eds. 121-154. New York: Guilford Press.

Hilton, M.E. 1988. Trends in U.S. drinking patterns: further evidence from the past 20 years. *British Journal of Addiction*. 83 (3): 269-278.

Jacobson, J. E, and J. S. W. Jacobson. 1999. Drinking moderately and pregnancy. *Alcohol Health and Research World*. 23: 25-34.

Jersild, Devon. 2001. *Happy Hours: Alcohol in a woman's life*. New York: HarperCollins Publishers.

Kaskutus, Lee A. 1992. An analysis of "Women For Sobriety." Ph.D. dissertation, Department of Public Health, University of California, Berkeley.

Katz, B. L. 1991. The psychological impact of stranger versus non stranger rape on victims' recovery. In *Acquaintance rape: The hidden crime*. A. Parrot and L. Bechhofer eds. 251-269. New York: John Wiley.

Kerr, A. S., and E. W. Hill. 1992. An exploratory study comparing ACoAs to Non-ACoAs on current family relationships. *Alcoholism Treatment Quarterly*. 9: 23-38.

Kirkpatrick, Jean. 1977. *Turnabout: new help for the woman alcoholic*. New York: Bantam Books.

_____1986. *Goodbye hangovers, hello life: self-help for women*. NewYork: Atheneum.

Koss, M. P, T. E. Dinero, C. A. Seibel, and S. L. Cox. 1988. Stranger and acquaintance rape: Are there differences in the victim's experience? *Psychology of Women Quarterly*. 12: 1-24.

Langeland, W., and C. Hangers. 1998. Child sexual and physical abuse and alcoholism. *Journal of Studies on Alcohol*. 59: 336-350.

La Rosa, J. H. 1990. Executive women and health: perceptions and practices. *American Journal of Public Health*. 80: 1450-1454.

Levesssue-Lopan, L. 1988. *Claiming reality: phenomenology and women's experience*. Rowman & Littlefield.

Levi, Andre A. 1996. Feminist reconstructions of identity in a self-help program: a study of two social movement organizations for incest survivors. Ph.D. dissertation, Ohio State University.

Lex, B. W. 1991. Gender differences and substance abuse. In *Advances in substance abuse: behavioral and biological research*. N. K. Mello, ed. 225-296. London: Jessica Kingsley Publishers.

Lorber, Judith and Susan A. Farrell. 1991. *The social construction of gender*. Newbury Park, CA. Sage Publications.

Lyon, D., and J. Greenberg. 1991. Evidence of codependency in women with an alcoholic parent: Helping out Mr. Wrong. *Journal of Personality and Social Psychology*. 61: 435-439.

Magura, M. and E. Shapiro. 1988. Alcohol Consumption and Divorce. *Journal of Divorce*. 12: 127-136.

Mäkelä, Klaus, Ilkka Arminen, Kim Bloomfield, Irmgard Eisenbach-Stangl, Karen Bergmark, Noriko Kurube, Nicoletta Mariolini, Ólasdóttir Hildigunnur, John H. Peterson, Mary Phillips, Jürgen Rehm, Robin Room, Pia Rosenqvist, Haydée Rosovsky, Kerstin Stenius, Grażyna Światkiewicz, Bohdan Woronowicz, and Antoni Zieliński.1996. *Alcoholics Anonymous as a mutual-help movement: A study in eight societies.* The University of Wisconsin Press.

Malin, H. Coakley, J., and Kaelber, C. 1982. An epidemiologic perspective on alcohol use and abuse in the United States. In: *Alcohol Consumption and Related Problems.* National Institute on Alcohol Abuse and Alcoholism. Alcohol and Health Monograph. No. 1. DHHS Pub. No. (ADM) 82-1190. Washington, DC: Supt. of Docs., U.S. Govt. Print. Off. 99-153.

McCaul, M. C., and J. Furst. 1994. Alcoholism treatment in the United States. *Alcohol Health and Research World.* 18: 257.

Miller, B. A., W. R. Downs, and D. M. Gondoli. 1989. Spousal violence among alcoholic women as compared to a random household sample of women. *Journal of Studies on Alcohol.* 50: 533-540.

Miller, B. A. and W. R. Downs. 1995. Violent victimization among women with alcohol problems. In *Recent developments in alcoholism and women.* M. Galanter, ed. 81-101. New York: Plenum Press.

Mills, C. Wright. 1959. *The Sociological Imagination.* New York. Oxford University Press.

Murphy, W. D., E. Coleman, E. Hoon, and C. Scott. 1980. Sexual dysfunction and treatment in alcoholic women. *Sexuality and Disability.* 3: 240-255.

Narcotics Anonymous. 1983. *Narcotics Anonymous: The basic text of recovery.* Van Nuys, CA. Narcotics Anonymous World Services, Inc.

National Institute on Alcohol Abuse and Alcoholism. 1998. *Drinking in the United States: Main Findings from the 1992 National Longitudinal Alcohol Epidemiologic Survey* (NLAES). U.S. Alcohol Epidemiologic Data Reference Manual. Vol. 6. Bethesda, Md: NIAAA; 1998.

National Institute on Drug Abuse. 1991. *Summary of Findings from the 1990 National Household Survey on Drug Abuse.* Rockville, MD: Division of Epidemiology and Prevention Research. DHHS Pub. No. (ADM) 91-1788.

National Institute on Drug Abuse. 2000. *Summary of Findings from the 1999 National Household Survey on Drug Abuse.* Office of Applied Studies, Series: H-12, DHHS Pub. No. (SMA) 00-3466, August 2000.

Pan, H. S. 1994. Predicting mild and severe husband-to-wife physical aggression. *Journal of Consulting and Clinical Psychology.* 62: 975-981.

Pape, P. 1986. Women and alcohol: the disgraceful discrepancy. *EAP Digest.* Sept./Oct.: 50-53.

Peluso, E. and L. Peluso. 1988. *Women and drugs: getting hooked, getting clean.* Minneapolis, MN: Compucare.

Plant, Moira. 1997. *Women and alcohol: contemporary and historical perspectives.* New York: Free Association Books.

Power and Estaugh. 1990. The role of family formation and dissolution in shaping drinking behavior in early adulthood. *British Journal of Addiction.* 86: 521-530.

Rapping, Elaine. 1996. *The culture of recovery: making sense of the self-help culture.* Boston: Beacon Press.

Reinharz, S. 1983. Experiential analysis: a contribution to feminist research. In *Theories of women's studies*. G. Bowles and R. D. Klein, eds.162-191. Boston: Routledge.

Royce, J. and D. Scratachley. 1996. *Alcoholism and other drug problems*. New York. The Free Press.

Sanders, Jolene. M. 2003. Twelve-step recovery and feminism: A study of empowerment among women in Alcoholics Anonymous. Ph.D. dissertation. Department of Sociology, American University, Washington, DC.

Schaef, Anne W. 1986. *Co-dependence: misunderstood-mistreated*. New York: HarperCollins.

____1987. *When Society Becomes an Addict*. CA.: Harper & Row.

Schultz, Alfred 1972. *The phenomenology of the social world*. Translated by George Walsh and Frederick Lehnert. Evanston, Ill.: Northwestern University Press, 1972, c1967.

Senchak, M., K. E. Leonard, B. W. Greene, and A. Carroll. 1995. Comparisons of adult children of alcoholic, divorced, and control parents in four outcome domains. *Psychology of Addictive Behaviors*. 9: 147-156.

Smith, Dorothy. 1978. *The everyday world as problematic: a feminist sociology*. Boston: Northeastern University Press.

Substance Abuse and Mental Health Services Administration (SAMHSA). 2001. Office of Applied Studies. *Polydrug Use among Treatment Admissions: 1998*. Treatment Episode Data Set (TEDS). Drug and Alcohol Services Information System. The DASIS Report.

Tallen, Bette S. 1995. Codependency; a feminist critique. In *Challenging codependency: feminist critiques*. M.. Babcock and C. McKay, eds. 169-176. University of Toronto Press.

Trevino, Alberto J. 1990. The feminine ethic of Alcoholics Anonymous: a study in the sociology of organizations. Ph.D. dissertation, Department of Sociology, Boston College, Boston, MA.

Ullman, A.D. and A. Orenstein. 1994. Why some children of alcoholics become alcoholics: emulation of the drinker. *Adolescence*. 29: 1-11.

United States Census Bureau. 2000a. Current population survey, March 2000. Special Populations Branch, Population Division. *Detailed occupational group of employed civilian population 16 years and over by sex*. Accessed November 15, 2001 at www.census.gov/population/socdemo/gender/ppl-121/tab12.txt.

____2000b. Current population survey, March 2000. Special Populations Branch, Population Division. *Marital status of the population 15 years and over by age and sex*. Accessed November 15, 2001 at http://www.census.gov/population/socdemo/gender/ppl-121/tab02.txt.

____2000c. Current population survey, March 2000. Special Populations Branch, Population Division. *Earnings of full-time, year-round workers 15 years and over in 1999 by sex*. Accessed November 15, 2001 at http://www.census.gov/population/socdemo/gender/ppl-121/tab13.txt.

____2000d. Current population survey, March 2000. Special Populations Branch, Population Division. *Educational attainment of the population 25 years and over by sex*. Accessed November 15, 2001 at http://www.census.gov/population/socdemo/gender/ppl-121/tab07.txt.

United States Department of Labor Women's Bureau. March, 2000. *Women at the millennium: Accomplishments and challenges ahead.* Publication 00-02. Accessed November 15, 2001 at http://www.dol.gov/dol/wb/public/wb-pubs/millennium52000.htm.

Van Den Bergh, Nan. 1991. Having bitten the apple: a feminist perspective on addictions. In *Feminist perspectives on addiction.* Nan N. Van Den Bergh, ed. 3-20. New York: Springer Publishing Co.

Vourakis, Christine H. 1989. The process of recovery of women in Alcoholics Anonymous: seeking groups "like me." Ph.D. dissertation, Department of Sociology, University of California, Berkeley, San Francisco.

Walters, Marianne. 1995. The codependent cinderella who loves too much ... fights back. In *Challenging codependency: feminist critiques.* M. Babcock and C. McKay, eds. 181-192. University of Toronto Press.

Walitzer, K.S. and K. J. Sher. 1996. A prospective study of self esteem and alcohol use disorders in young adulthood: Evidence for gender differences. *Alcoholism-Clinical and Experimental Research.* 20 (6): 1118-1124.

Weinberg, N.Z., T. E. Dielman, W. Mandell, and J.T. Shope. 1994. Parental drinking and gender factors on the prediction of early adolescent alcohol use. *International Journal of the Addictions.* 29: 89-104.

Wilsnack R. W., S. C. Wilsnack, and A. D. Klassen. 1984. Women's drinking and drinking problems patterns from a 1981 national survey. *American Journal of Public Health.* 74 (11): 1231-1238.

Wilsnack, R.W. and R. Cheloha. 1987. Women's roles and problem drinking across the lifespan. *Social Problems.* 34 (3): 231-248.

Wilsnack, R., S. Wilsnack, and S. Hiller-Sturmhofel. 1994. How women drink: epidemiology of women's drinking and problem drinking. *Alcohol, Health and Research World.* 18 (3): 173-181.

Windle, M. 1994. Substance use, risky behaviors, and victimization among a US national adolescent sample. *Addiction.* 89: 175-182.

Worth, Dooley. 1991. American Women and Polydrug Abuse. In *Alcohol and Drugs are Women's Issues.* Paula Roth ed. Women's Action Alliance and The Scarecrow Press, Inc. Metuchen, N.J., & London

Index

A
abuse: alcohol, 22-23, 30, 64; drug, 5, 22, 31-32, 41, 58, 61; parental, 5; past, 21, 28-30, 58; physical, 31; sexual, 2, 9, 12, 18, 28-29, 31, 43, 130; substance, 7, 15-17, 29, 33, 43, 45, 58
accidents, 31, 38
addiction treatment, 1, 129
adult children, 5, 34
Adult Children of Alcoholics (ACA), 45, 58, 61-62, 77
agnostic, 79
Al-Anon, 45, 58, 60-62, 64-65, 69, 77, 130-131
alcohol: abuse, 22-23, 30, 64 (*see also under* abuse); addiction, 2, 14, 28-29, 41-42, 65; dependence, 22-23
Alcoholics Anonymous (AA): culture, 48, 55, 65, 99, 101, 106 (*see also under* culture); founders (*see* Bill w. and Dr. Bob); groups, 8, 17, 103; literature, 16, 46, 55, 68, 79, 92, 98-100, 129; meetings (*see* mixed meetings and women-only meetings); members, 7-9, 25, 32, 59-60, 70, 72, 75, 81-82, 87, 98, 101-104, 107, 111, 113; membership survey, 7, 19, 23-25, 27, 43, 46-47, 58, 104; organization, 1, 4-5, 7-8, 10, 102-103; program, 72, 80, 98, 106; sample, 24, 26-27, 43, 48, 64, 107, 118, 120
alcoholism. *See under* alcohol
amends: list, 82, 94; make 19, 74, 81-82, 90, 92-93, 95, 128
American Psychiatric Association (APA), 22
American Society of Addiction Medicine (ASAM), 17
arrests, 38

assault, 9, 12, 28-30, 53. See *also* abuse

B
barbiturates, 31, 41. *See also* prescription drugs
Beattie, Melody, 12
Big Book, 17, 55, 63, 72, 79, 81-82, 85, 90, 97-98
Bill W., 49, 65

C
Catholic, 79, 107-108, 112
character defects, 12, 58, 81, 87-90, 07, 128
Chemical Dependency Anonymous (CDA), 61-62
Christian, 4, 74, 107, 111
cocaine, 31, 41-42
Co-Dependent Anonymous (CoDA), 45, 61-62, 64, 130-131
compulsion, 7, 63, 71, 75, 88, 133
control issues, 77
"conscious contact," 56, 97-98
consciousness-raising groups, 3, 10
culture: of AA, 18, 123; of recovery, 7, 13, 123, 131, 138; patriarchal, 10, 121; twelve step, 11, 13, 64, 115, 129, 131

D
defense mechanism, 88
denial, 36, 39, 68-69, 72-74, 83, 89, 129, 131
Denzin, Norman, 13, 49, 52, 131-132, 136
depression, 2, 9, 31, 34-37, 43, 57, 63
disease, 1-2, 8, 19, 37, 71, 73, 86, 91, 128; family, 30, 60; model, 23; of addiction, 9; of alcoholism, 36, 69-70
divorce, 24-25, 31, 38-40, 42, 133
dysfunctional families, 5

drug abusing parents, 32
Dr. Bob, 49, 65, 75, 103
driving while intoxicated (DWI), 38. *See also* accidents
dual addiction, 28, 40, 61

E
empowerment: collective, 116; feminist (*see under* feminist); individual, 127, 134; personal empowerment, 43, 123, 125, 127, 130, 133
enable, 7, 60, 130

F
family addiction, 30
fellowship, 8, 61-62, 71, 98, 123
feminist: activities, 14, 122; consciousness, 3-4, 14, 17, 116-118, 121-123, 131-133; empowerment, 3, 13-14, 116, 118, 130; indicators, 120; methodology, 16
Fetal Alcohol Syndrome and Effects (FAS/E), 2
forgiveness, 90-91, 95-96, 101, 109

G
gender roles, 4, 115-118, 123
General Service Office (GSO), 9
General Service Representative (GSR), 101-102
General Social Survey (GSS), 17-19, 107-108, 110-112, 116-117, 120-121
God, 4, 40, 53, 74-75, 108-112, 119, 126-133
gratitude, 101, 123-124

H
health, 38, 43, 45, 56-59, 63, 72, 124
"hitting bottom," 71-72
higher power, 4, 56, 74-79, 97, 104, 108-112, 126-129, 133
homelessness, 40
honest, 52-55, 83-88, 93, 95

I
inner peace, 127. *See also* serenity

K
Kirkpatrick, Jean, 3-4, 66

L
liberal feminism, 4, 14

M
Mann, Marty, 9
marijuana, 31, 42
meditation, 57, 98-99, 110-112. *See also* prayer
Mills, C. Wright, 15
mixed AA meetings, 48
mental illness, 36, 111
moral inventory, 19, 74, 81-87, 128
mutual aid society, 49

N
Narcotics Anonymous (NA), 61-62
National Household Survey on Drug Abuse, 22
National Institute of Mental Health, 43
National Institute on Alcohol Abuse and Alcoholism, 23, 30
National Institute on Drug Abuse, 22, 58
National Longitudinal Alcohol Epidemiology Survey (NLAES), 23
newcomer, 69-71, 102-103

O
Overeaters Anonymous (OA), 61-62

P
personal growth, 10, 123, 133
phenomenological feminism, 14
powerlessness, 60, 63, 67-69, 71-72, 74, 128
prayer, 98-100, 107, 110-113, 127, 129
prescription drugs, 31, 41
Protestant, 79, 107-108, 111
psychiatrist, 58

R
Rapping, Elaine, 11, 13, 64, 78,
    121, 130
recovery: culture (see *under*
    culture); groups 45, 131;
    identity 131-132; ideology, 13,
    131; issues, 10; language 129;
    movement, 4, 11, 129;
    philosophy 7; process, 6-7, 13,
    56, 65, 85, 87-88; program,
    111, 113
relapse, 40, 46, 58, 69-72, 82
relationships: healthy, 57, 59, 127,
    129; improved, 123, 125;
    intimate, 132; personal, 56, 65
religion, 18, 75-76, 78-79, 106-
    107, 109
responsibility, 63, 77-78, 84, 94,
    102-103, 124

S
second-wave feminism, 3, 13, 19
self-blame, 94. See also shame
self-esteem, 3, 10, 12, 30, 66, 86-
    87, 89, 123-125, 127, 130-131
serenity, 46, 124, 126; prayer, 111,
    127
Schultz, Alfred, 15
shame, 3, 8, 12, 30, 35, 37-38, 86-
    87, 89, 92, 94-95, 128. See also
    self-blame
shortcomings, 82, 88-90, 95, 125.
    See also character defects
self-centered fear, 84-85, 87
service work, 101
slip, 69, 105. See also relapse
Smith, Dorothy, 6
sobriety: early, 56; in AA, 18, 45-
    46; maintaining, 101, 106; new
    found, 127; time, 46; women
    in, 49; years of, 32, 46, 53, 65,
    70, 76, 133
spiritual: activities, 113; aspects,
    55-56; awakening, 7, 82, 91,
    100-101, 106; awareness, 126;
    beliefs, 107; condition, 97,
    100; culture, 100;
    development, 4, 57, 67, 100,
    126; enlightenment, 4;
    experience, 19, 106; growth,

127; life, 57, 103, 124, 126;
    literature, 99; matters, 51;
    needs, 57; practices, 98-99,
    129; principles, 18, 100;
    processes, 128; program, 60,
    67, 99, 106, 108, 111, 113,
    127; recovery, 131
sponsor, 46, 49-50, 70-71, 82, 84,
    92, 98, 103-106
suicidal thoughts, 31, 36
surrender, 18, 67, 69, 71-73, 75-80,
    86, 89, 115

T
The Culture of Recovery
    (Rapping), 11
therapist, 45, 58, 62, 65, 69. See
    also psychiatrist
trust, 10, 51, 53, 78, 102, 133
Twelve and Twelve, 81
twelve-step movement, 5, 11-14,
    18, 45, 123, 130, 132
Twelve Steps: Eighth Step, 12, 19,
    90-91, 94, 96-97, 128; Eighth-
    Step list, 92-93; Eleventh Step,
    98-100,111, 113, 129;
    Eleventh-Step activities, 129;
    Fifth Step, 58, 81-82, 88, 97;
    First Step, 68-69, 71-72, 74-75,
    77, 80, 86, 128; Fourth Step,
    12, 19, 82-89, 91-92, 95-97,
    128; Fourth-Step inventory, 81,
    87; Ninth Step, 81, 90, 126-
    127; Second Step, 74-75, 86;
    Seventh Step, 82; Sixth Step,
    58, 82, 88; Tenth Step, 97-98;
    Third Step, 78-80, 86-87, 90,
    109, 127-128; Twelfth Step,
    49, 67, 103-104, 113; Twelfth-
    Step activities, 101-102, 106,
    129; Twelfth-Step work, 101-
    103

U
U.S. Census, 17, 19, 25

V
victimization, 2, 3, 29

W
"war on drugs," 6
women-only meetings, 9-10, 16,
    45-48, 99; attend, 14, 46, 49-
50, 52, 65, 129; prefer, 50-52,
    54, 65; support, 48
Women for Sobriety, 3, 62, 64, 66
"wreckage of the past," 95

About the Book

Can a recovery program like Alcoholics Anonymous inadvertently discourage women from seeking treatment? Are there ways that it can more effectively contribute to their sobriety? Combining individual personal narratives with statistical data, Jolene Sanders offers valuable insight into how women adapt the twelve-step program and interact with the masculine culture of AA in ways that allow them to conquer addiction and take control of their lives.

Jolene M. Sanders is assistant professor of sociology at Hood College.